南無本師釋迦牟尼佛

相德人上公宣

慈悲普度信者得救成正覺

過化存神禮之獲福悟無生

The Venerable Master Hsuan Hua

His kindness and compassion cross over all; Believers are liberated and perfect the Right Enlightenment.
Transforming beings wherever he goes, his spirit remains intact;
Those who venerate him obtain blessings and awaken to the Unproduced.

宣公上人德相❋
The Venerable Master Hsuan Hua

❈楞嚴經淺釋（書、錄音帶）---宣化上人講述
佛經翻譯委員會 出版
The *Shurangama Sutra* with Commentary by
the Venerable Master Hsuan Hua:
Books and tapes published by the Buddhist Text Translation Society

將佛陀的教誨祖師的風範言行傳布四方，佛經的翻譯是極重要的功作。迄今，國際譯經學院已將宣公上人講述的楞嚴經、華嚴經、法華經、金剛經、六祖壇經等大乘經典以英文、中文、西班牙文及越南文出版於世，計約一百五十餘部，並發行萬佛城月刊---金剛菩提海。

In order to propagate the Buddha's teachings and make known the exemplary words and deeds of the patriarchs, it is of utmost importance to translate the Buddhist Sutras. The International Translation Institute has already published over a hundred and fifty volumes of the Venerable Master Hua's commentaries on the Sutras, including the *Shurangama Sutra*, the *Flower Adornment Sutra*, the *Dharma Flower Sutra*, the *Vajra Sutra*, the *Sixth Patriarch Sutra*, and other Mahayana Sutras, in the languages of Chinese, English, Spanish, and Vietnamese. It also distributes the *The Buddhist Monthly--Vajra Bodhi Sea*.

萬佛聖城⸻
黑暗中的明燈

The City of Ten Thousand Buddhas:
--- *A Bright Light in the Darkness*

宣演正法萬佛城

現在未來永不停

菩提泉湧甘露水

般若雲封龍樹林

白鶴麋鹿聞風化

玄鳥迦陵和音雅

法界眾生歸依處

大方廣佛華嚴經

The City of Ten Thousand Buddhas proclaims the Proper Dharma
Now and in the future, never stopping.
Sweet dew water flows from the spring of Bodhi
Dragon-tree Forest is sealed with clouds of Prajna
White cranes and deer are influenced by example;
Blackbirds and kalavinkas sing in harmony.
The place of refuge of the living beings of the Dharma Realm,
The Great Means Expansive Buddha Flower Adornment Sutra.

❋萬佛聖城鳥瞰全景
A bird's-eye view of the City of Ten Thousand Buddhas

Dharma Realm Buddhist Association
City of Ten Thousand Buddhas
Dharma Realm Buddhist University

法界佛教總會
萬佛聖城
法界佛教大學

❋萬佛聖城舉行傳戒大典
The Ordination Ceremony at the City of Ten Thousand Buddhas

❋南北傳本是一家人--上人率團赴英國訪問
The Northern and Southern Traditions of Buddhism are basically the
same family. The Venerable Master leads a delegation to England.

❊孝是做人的根本，上人提倡敬老尊賢活動
Filial piety is the foundation of humanity—the Venerable Master promotes "respecting the elderly and honoring the worthy."

❊漢堡大學學生訪問萬佛聖城
Students of Humboldt University visit the City of 10,000 Buddhas.

※萬佛聖城男女校舉行升旗典禮
Flag-raising ceremony at the boys' and girls' schools
at the City of Ten Thousand Buddhas

宣化上人開示錄

（四）

Venerable Master Hua's
Talks on Dharma

Volume Four

宣化上人開示錄

（四）

英 譯

佛經翻譯委員會

出 版

法界佛教總會
佛經翻譯委員會
法界佛教大學

Venerable Master Hua's
Talks on Dharma

Volume Four

English translation by the
Buddhist Text Translation Society

Buddhist Text Translation Society
Dharma Realm Buddhist University
Dharma Realm Buddhist Association
Burlingame. California U.S.A.

Published and translated by:

Buddhist Text Translation Society
1777 Murchison Drive,
Burlingame, CA 94010-4504

1995 Buddhist Text Translation Society,
Dharma Realm Buddhist University,
Dharma Realm Buddhist Association

First Chinese edition published 1984,
Dharma Realm Buddhist Books Distribution Society

First bilingual edition 1995
(Second Chinese edition, First English edition)

03 02 01 00 99 98 97 96 95   10 9 8 7 6 5 4 3 2 1

ISBN 0-88139-028-3

Notes : Pinyin is used for the romanization of Chinese
      words, except for proper names which retain
      familiar romanizations.

Addresses of the Dharma Realm Buddhist Association's branch
offices are listed at the back of this book.

佛經翻譯委員會八項基本守則
The Eight Guidelines of
The Buddhist Text Translation Society

1. 從事翻譯工作者不得抱有個人的名利。
   A volunteer must free him/herself from the motives of personal fame and reputation.

2. 從事翻譯工作者不得貢高我慢，必須以虔誠恭敬的態度來工作。
   A volunteer must cultivate an attitude free from arrogance and conceit.

3. 從事翻譯工作者不得自讚毀他。
   A volunteer must refrain from aggrandizing his/her work and denigrating that of others.

4. 從事翻譯工作者不得自以為是，對他人作品吹毛求疵。
   A volunteer must not establish him/herself as the standard of correctness and suppress the work of others with his or her fault-finding.

5. 從事翻譯工作者必須以佛心為己心。
   A volunteer must take the Buddha-mind as his/her own mind.

6. 從事翻譯工作者必須運用擇法眼來辨別正確的道理。
   A volunteer must use the wisdom of Dharma-Selecting Vision to determine true principles.

7. 從事翻譯工作者必須懇請十方大德長老來印證其翻譯。
   A volunteer must request Virtuous Elders in the ten directions to certify his/her translations.

8. 從事翻譯工作者之作品在獲得印證之後，必須努力弘揚流通經、律、論以及佛書以光大佛教。
   A volunteer must endeavor to propagate the teachings by printing Sutras, Shastra texts, and Vinaya texts when the translations are certified as being correct.

目　錄

2　　天竺取經的玄奘大師

22　　參禪要迴光返照

28　　禪堂是選佛的道場

36　　什麼是無心道人？

40　　參禪是行六度波羅蜜

46　　要修無相的功德

52　　虛雲老和尚出家的因緣

70　　宣化老禪師出家的因緣

88　　果佐行者出家的因緣

96　　果舜行者出家的因緣

106　　修道的六大宗旨

114　　久參自然會開悟

118　　修道不要爭第一

126　　修道目的為成佛

Contents

The Story of Great Master Hsuan Tsang, Who Went to
India in Search of Sutras   3

To Investigate Chan, We Must Look Within Ourselves   23

The Meditation Hall Is a Way-place
Where Buddhas Are Selected   29

What Is a "Person of the
Way Who Is Without Thought"?   37

Chan Meditation Involves Practicing the Six Paramitas   41

Cultivate Merit and Virtue without Marks   47

The Story of Venerable Master Hsu Yun's
Leaving the Home-life   53

The Story of the Venerable Master Hsuan Hua's
Leaving the Home-life   71

The Story of Cultivator Guo Zuo's
Leaving the Home-life   89

The Story of Cultivator Guo Shun's
Leaving the Home-life   97

The Six Great Guidelines for Cultivating the Way   107

Long-term Meditation Will Naturally
Bring You to Enlightenment   115

Don't Compete to be Number One As You
Cultivate the Way   119

Our Goal in Cultivating the Way Is Buddhahood   127

132　停止你的妄想吧！

136　入定不是睡覺

142　《楞嚴經》是偽經嗎？

150　要修般若波羅蜜多

160　修道人不可打妄語

166　修道人要受苦

172　去妄心存真心

178　迷時師度，悟時自度

186　參禪要克服痛關

192　怎樣才夠資格參禪？

194　一身病苦從何來？

200　貪著境界會招魔

206　四禪天的境界

210　參禪的祕訣

214　金剛王寶劍斬妄想

219　附錄

Why Don't You Stop Your Idle Thoughts?   133

Entering Samadhi Is Not the Same as Sleeping   137

Is the *Shurangama Sutra* an Inauthentic Sutra?   143

Cultivate the Prajnaparamita!
(Perfection of wisdom)   151

Cultivators of the Way Must Not Tell Lies   161

Cultivators of the Way Should Undergo Suffering   167

Get Rid of False Thoughts;
Hold onto True Thoughts   173

Confused, You Are Saved by a Teacher;
Awakened, You Save Yourself   179

In Chan Meditation, We Must Pass Through
the Gate of Pain   187

What Makes One Qualified to Practice
Chan Meditaiton?   193

Where Do Illnesses Originate?   195

Attachment to States Leads to Demonic Possession   201

The States of the Four Dhyana Heavens   207

The Secret to Success in Chan Meditation   211

The Vajra-King Jeweled Sword Cuts Through
Idle Thoughts   215

Appendix   219

開 經 偈
Verse for Opening a Sutra

無 上 甚 深 微 妙 法
The unsurpassed, deep, profound,
subtle, wonderful Dharma,

百 千 萬 劫 難 遭 遇
In hundreds of thousands of millions of eons,
is difficult to encounter;

我 今 見 聞 得 受 持
I now see and hear it, receive and uphold it,

願 解 如 來 眞 實 義
And I vow to fathom the Tathagata's
true and actual meaning.

天竺取經的玄奘大師

寧向西天一步死，不願東土一步生。

玄奘法師生於隋文帝仁壽二年（西元六○一年），河南陳留人，俗姓陳，幼年即有過人的智慧，七歲時便開始讀五經。在十三歲那年，隨其二兄長捷法師到洛陽淨土寺出家，誦習經典。隋朝制度，凡是出家修道之人，必須經過考試合格，頒發證書（度牒），才有資格做沙彌。當時正逢洛陽度僧，玄奘法師年幼，不能參加考試。他在考場門前徘徊，望之興嘆！而被主考官鄭善果發現，認為是佛門龍象，故特別破例度之。

二十歲受具足戒之後，他就到處參訪善知識，發現眾師所說，與經典頗有歧異，令人無所適從。尤其《十七地論》，見解不同。乃發願到天竺（即印度）研究，以解其惑。

由於赴天竺路途，要經過崇山峻嶺、崎嶇不平的

The Story of Great Master Hsuan Tsang, Who Went to India in Search of Sutras

I would rather die while making one last step towards the West, than live by retreating one step towards the East.

Dharma Master Hsuan Tsang was born in the second year of the reign period Renshou of the Emperor Wen of the Sui Dynasty (A.D. 601). His home was in Honan Province, Chenliu County, and his lay surname was Chen. Even as a young boy, his wisdom surpassed his peers. At age seven, he began to study the Five Classics, and at age thirteen, he travelled with his second elder brother, the Dharma Master Chang Jie, to Pure Land Monastery in Luoyang to leave the home-life and study and recite Sutras. According to the laws of the Sui Dynasty, people who wished to leave the home-life had to pass an examination and receive certification before they could qualify to become Shramaneras (novice monks). The two of them reached Luoyang just as the clerks were enrolling candidates for Sangha membership. Dharma Master Hsuan Tsang was too young, and was not qualified to take the examination. He anxiously paced back and forth outside the door of the examination hall, sighing in consternation. But then he was discovered by the supervisor of the examinations, Mr. Shanguo Zheng. The man recognized the boy as a potential asset to Buddhism, and made a special exception to the standards, in order to admit him into the Sangha.

After receiving full ordination at age twenty, Dharma Master Hsuan Tsang travelled about, learning from Good and Wise

山道，所以玄奘法師在未啓程之前，先練習爬山越嶺的技術，先用桌子、凳子之類物品，堆成假山，從這邊爬到那邊，再從那邊爬到這邊。這樣一天練習多次，後來自己感覺爬山的技術不錯，又到山上去實地練習，約有一年經驗，技術方臻熟練。

於是上表，申請到天竺取經。當時（唐朝）的法令，禁止人民出境，所以未獲唐太宗批准。但是玄奘法師已拿定主意，無論批准與否，他決定赴天竺一行，所以最後不得不私自出境。

從長安出發，隻身向西行，經過一個山洞，見洞口有蝙蝠糞，當時玄奘法師想：「這洞中一定無人住，否則不會有這麼多的蝙蝠糞。」好奇的心理使他向洞中走去，在不遠的地方，他發現一個怪物，頭髮都結在一起，小鳥在上面做窩，窩中小鳥吱吱哇哇在叫，這怪物臉上的塵土很厚，好像石頭人一般。玄奘法師走近仔細一看，原來是位老修行，已經入定。玄奘法師用引磬給他開靜，令他出定，一會兒，這位老修行開始動彈。

Advisors. He discovered that the teachings of the various masters differed in large measure from the Sutra texts in the Canon, and as a result, no one knew where to turn. This was especially the case with the *Shastra on the Seventeen Stages,* which produced many different opinions. Master Hsuan Tsang thus made a vow to go to India to investigate the Dharma, in order to resolve his doubts.

Since the route to India passed over craggy peaks and tall passes, Master Hsuan Tsang prepared for the trek by learning the art of mountain climbing. He piled chairs, tables, and other furniture into miniature mountains, and then hopped back and forth from one pile to the next, practicing many rounds each day. Once his skill was sufficient, he ventured outside for first-hand training on real mountains. After a year of practice, he became quite proficient.

At this point, he applied for permission to travel to India to obtain the Sutras. As the laws of the Tang Dynasty forbade civilian travel across the border, the Tang Emperor Taizong (Li Shimin) refused his request. However, Master Hsuan Tsang was resolute. With or without permission, he was determined to make the trip to India. Finally he was forced to secretly cross the border.

While heading west alone from the capital, Changan, Master Hsuan Tsang passed by a mountain cave with piles of bat-droppings by the entrance. It occurred to him that nobody lived in the cave, or else the bat-dung could not have piled up outside the cave entrance. Full of curiosity, he ventured into the cave to explore, and not far from the entrance, he discovered a monster. Its hair had been woven together atop its head, and birds had made a nest there. The baby birds were chirping and squeaking from the next. A thick layer of

玄奘法師便問他：「老同參！你坐在這裏做什麼啊？」

老修行的嘴巴，動了幾次，才發出聲音來：「我等紅陽佛（釋迦牟尼佛）出世，我好幫他弘揚佛法。」

玄奘法師說：「老同參！釋迦牟尼佛已經入涅槃了。」

老修行一聽，很驚訝地問：「釋迦牟尼佛在什麼時候出世？」

玄奘法師說：「在一千多年前，出現於世。佛滅度已經很久了！」

老修行又說：「釋迦牟尼佛入涅槃，那麼我還是入定，等白陽佛（彌勒佛）出世，我再幫他弘揚佛法吧！」

玄奘大師說：「老同參！你不要再入定了，等彌勒佛出世時，你又要錯過機會，不如現在跟我到震旦，將來我取經回來，你好幫我弘揚佛法。」

老修行一想，言之有理，於是答應大師的要求。

玄奘法師對他說：「你的身體太舊了，你要換一

dirt on the creature's face gave it the look of a stone statue. Master Hsuan Tsang drew nearer for a closer look, only to discover that it was an old cultivator who had long since entered samadhi. Ringing a handbell, he brought the old cultivator out of samadhi. A moment passed, then the old cultivator began to stir a bit.

The Great Master said, "Fellow cultivator! What are you doing, sitting here like this?"

The old cultivator had to wiggle his jaw a few times before he could make any sound. He answered, "I'm waiting here for the Red Yang Buddha (Shakyamuni Buddha) to come into the world, so I can help him propagate the Buddhadharma."

Master Hsuan Tsang replied, "Fellow cultivator! Shakyamuni Buddha has already entered Nirvana!"

The old cultivator was amazed by this news, and asked, "When did Shakyamuni Buddha appear in the world?"

Master Hsuan Tsang replied, "He was born over a thousand years ago, and he has already entered Nirvana for quite a long time."

The old cultivator said, "In that case, I'll go back into samadhi, and wait for the White Yang Buddha (Maitreya Buddha) to appear in the world, and then help him to propagate the Buddhadharma."

"Fellow cultivator! There's no need for you to go back into samadhi and wait for Maitreya Buddha to appear in the world," said the Master. "You'll surely miss him, too. It'd be better for you to go with me to China, and when I return from my pilgrimage for Sutras, you'll be able help me propagate the Buddhadharma."

The old cultivator thought it over and decided that Master Hsuan Tsang's suggestion was quite reasonable, so he agreed to it.

個新的房子。你到長安去，看到黃色琉璃瓦的屋子，你就到那裏去投胎，等我從天竺（印度）取經回來，我再來找你。」於是老修行辭別玄奘法師，二人便分手，一向東走，一向西行，各自奔前程。

玄奘法師經過跋山涉水，迭遭災難而不灰心。曾經誓言：

> 寧向西天一步死，
> 不願東土一步生。

這種爲法忘軀的精神，實在偉大！所以他能完成偉大的事業，對中國佛教有所貢獻，並且創立了「唯識宗」。所謂「見賢思齊」，我們希望成就道業，應該以玄奘法師爲寶鑑，做爲模範，向他看齊，把本有的智慧現出來，爲佛教貢獻一分力量。

一日復一日，玄奘法師餐風宿露，披星戴月，向西前進。他抱著堅忍不拔的意志，不到目的地（天竺），決不休息。所謂「有志者事竟成」，經過千辛萬苦，在路上行走三年，終於到達天竺的

Dharma Master Hsuan Tsang told him, "Your body is too old and decrepit; you should change it for a new one. Why don't you go to Changan, to the house with yellow roof-tiles, and be reborn there. When I return from my trip to India to obtain Sutras, I'll go to find you." The two of them said goodbye, one heading east and one going west, each of them on his mission.

Dharma Master Hsuan Tsang scaled peaks and forded rivers, encountering numerous calamities and trials without losing his nerve. At one point he made a vow, saying,

I would rather die while making one last step towards the West, than live by retreating one step towards the East.

His selfless courage in quest of the Dharma was truly noble. As a result of his momentous work, he made a magnificent contribution to Chinese Buddhism, and he established the Consciousness Only (Weishi) School. A maxim tells us to "Imitate worthy models." In our hope to accomplish our work of cultivation, we can take Dharma Master Hsuan Tsang as our worthy model and guide. We can measure ourselves by his example, uncover our inherent wisdom, and give our share of strength to Buddhism as he did.

From one day to the next, Master Hsuan Tsang endured the hardships of travel, eating and sleeping outdoors. He was constantly exposed to the elements on his journey to the West. His resolve was unshakable: until he reached his goal—India—he would never rest. As the motto goes: "Perseverance brings success." He underwent a myriad bitter hardships; and his pilgrimage took over three years, bringing him finally to India's Buddhist University, Nalanda Monastery, where he became a

佛教大學（那爛陀寺），拜戒賢論師為師（當時天竺唯識學權威），專學《十七地論》及《瑜珈論》等經典。學成歸國，路經曲女城，為戒日王所請，在該城成立辯論大會，參加者有十八國的國王，以及大乘、小乘、婆羅門和外道等，約有六千人，盛況空前。大師為論主，稱揚大乘，序作論義，懸於會場門外，並言：「如改一字，願拜他為師。」經過十八天，無人能改，最後勝利，名揚五天竺，無人不知，無人不曉這位大名鼎鼎的玄奘法師。

貞觀十九年（西元六四五年）正月二十四日，玄奘法師回到長安，當時僧俗出迎者有數十萬人。唐太宗派相國梁國公、房玄齡等為代表，歡迎玄奘法師。後於弘福寺，從事翻譯經典工作。

玄奘法師在天竺留學十二年（在路上往返耽誤五年），成為中國留學生的祖師。他取回的經典有五百二十篋，計有六百多部。他將全部經典貢獻給國家，特蒙皇帝召見，嘉獎一番。

玄奘法師見到唐太宗便向皇帝賀喜：「恭喜陛下。」

disciple of India's authority in Consciousness Only, Shastra Master Shilabhadra (Moral and Worthy). He specialized in the study of the two treatises, the *Shastra on the Seventeen Stages* and the *Yogacharyabhumi Shastra*, and other Sutras. After he finished his studies, on his way back to China, he passed through the city of Kanyakudja. At the invitation of King Shiladitya, he organized a great debate, the participants of which numbered over six thousand people. Among them were the kings of eighteen countries, monks of both Great and Small Vehicles, Brahmans, and externalists, all coming together in an unprecedented gathering. As the host of the debate, the Great Master praised and propagated the Great Vehicle, posting his treatise out by the main entrance. He challenged all comers, claiming that if anyone could improve his treatise by even a single word, he would bow to that person and become his disciple. Eighteen days passed, and no one could change even one word of the text. He won the great debate, and his name spread throughout India's five kingdoms. There was not a person who did not hear of his accomplishment. Such was the peerless reputation of the Great Master Hsuan Tsang.

In the nineteenth year of the Zhenguan reign period (A.D. 645) of the Tang Dynasty, on the twenty-fourth day of the first lunar month, he returned to Changan, and was welcomed by several hundreds of thousands of Sangha members and citizens. Emperor Taizong of the Tang Dynasty sent high-ranking cabinet ministers Liang Guogong, Fang Xuanling, and others as representatives to welcome Dharma Master Hsuan Tsang. Later, he was taken to Hongfu (Vast Blessings) Monastery, where he began translating the Sutras.

Dharma Master Hsuan Tsang's pilgrimage to study in India took over twelve years, five of which were spent in the journey back and forth. He became the "patriarch" of all overseas students from

11

唐太宗覺得莫明其妙，就問：「喜從何來？」

玄奘法師說：「陛下得一位太子。」

唐太宗有丈二金剛摸不著頭腦的感覺，便說：「沒有啊！」

玄奘法師心想：「明明指示老修行來投胎，怎會沒有呢？」於是在定中觀察。哎呀！老修行搞不清楚，投錯胎了，跑到尉遲恭家裏去了。玄奘法師將這段因緣，向唐太宗報告。

唐太宗說：「原來如此，那你就去度他吧！」

玄奘法師便去找尉遲恭，說明來意。他一見尉遲恭的姪子，心生歡喜，因爲窺基的身體，非常魁偉，相貌堂堂，一表人才，是載法之器。於是他開門見山便說：「你跟我出家吧！」窺基一聽，莫名其妙，不悅地說：「你說什麼？叫我出家，豈有此理！」轉身就走了。

玄奘法師只好與唐太宗商量，成就這段因緣。於是乎皇帝下旨，要尉遲恭的姪子出家，尉遲恭一

China. The Sutra texts he brought back numbered five hundred and twenty cases and comprised over six hundred works. He offered all the Sutras as a gift to the nation. The Emperor summoned him for an special audience and conferred praise and favor upon him.

Master Hsuan Tsang said to Emperor Taizong, "Congratulations, your Majesty!"

The comment struck the Emperor as quite unusual "What am I being congratulated for?" he asked.

"A son has been born to Your Highness."

The Emperor's face bore an expression of utter bewilderment. "No, that's not so!" he said.

Dharma Master Hsuan Tsang thought, "I told that old cultivator clearly to come be reborn here; how could he have gone wrong?" He promptly entered samadhi and perceived that the old cultivator had entered the wrong house and been reborn to the wrong family. He had accidentally been born to the family of Wei Chigong, the War Minister. Dharma Master Hsuan Tsang then reported this turn of events in full to the Emperor.

"Oh, in that case," said Emperor Taizong, "Just go and save him."

Dharma Master Hsuan Tsang called on General Wei Chigong and explained the reason for his visit. When the Master saw Wei Chigong's nephew, he was delighted, because the young man's physique was quite imposing, and his countenance was dignified. He looked thoroughly talented, fit to be a vessel of the Dharma. Master Hsuan Tsang came right to the point and said, "Come and leave the home-life with me!" The nephew was astounded, and answered unhappily, "What did you say? Leave home? Impossible!" And he turned and left.

接到聖旨，便叫姪子出家。窺基嚴辭拒絕，說：「豈有此理！皇帝怎麼可以叫我出家？我還沒玩夠哪！我要去和皇帝講道理。」第二天尉遲恭帶著姪子來見皇帝。

窺基一來便說：「陛下要我出家，可以！可是我有三個條件。」

唐太宗一聽就說：「你要多少個條件都可以。」

窺基就說了：「我最歡喜喝酒，我不能沒有酒，無論我到什麼地方，都要有一車的酒跟著。」

唐太宗心想：「出家人是戒酒，可是玄奘法師告訴我，不管什麼條件都答應。」於是就說了：「好！我答應你。第二個條件呢？」

窺基說：「我知道出家人不可以吃肉，可是我歡喜吃肉，無論我到什麼地方，後面都要有一車新鮮的肉跟著。」

唐太宗說：「我答應你。第三個條件呢？」

窺基沒想到皇帝會答應他的條件，於是他接著又說：「出家人是不可以有太太的，可是我離不開

Dharma Master Hsuan Tsang had no alternative but to request Emperor Taizong to lend a hand in order to bring this event to a successful conclusion. Thereupon, the Emperor ordered Minister Wei Chigong's nephew to leave the home-life. When the Minister received this imperial order, he told his nephew to leave home. But his nephew defiantly refused, saying, "Ridiculous! How can the Emperor tell me to leave the home-life? I haven't played around enough yet. I'm going to have a talk with the Emperor." The next day, Wei Chigong took his nephew to see the Emperor.

As soon as they arrived, the nephew said, "If the Emperor wants me to leave the home-life, I'll do it, but I have three conditions."

The Emperor replied, "You can set as many conditions as you want."

The nephew said, "I love to drink wine, and I can't live without it. Wherever I go, I must bring along a cart of wine."

Emperor Taizhong thought, "Monks are supposed to abstain from wine, but Dharma Master Hsuan Tsang told me to agree to any condition he set." So he said, "Fine. I grant your request. What is your second condition?"

The nephew said, "I know that monks are not allowed to eat meat, but I like to eat meat, and I must have a cart of fresh meat to follow me wherever I go."

The Emperor said, "I will grant you this. What is your third condition?"

The nephew hadn't expected the Emperor to agree to his demands. He continued, "Monks cannot have wives. However, I cannot renounce women. Wherever I go, there must be a cart of beautiful women to accompany me." He thought to himself, "The Emperor will never agree to this."

女人，無論我到什麼地方，必須有一車的女人跟著。」他心想：「這個條件，皇帝無論如何一定不會答應的。」

唐太宗心想：「哎呀！這怎麼能答應呢？可是玄奘法師已經囑咐我，不管什麼條件一定都要答應。」所以就說了：「好！我完全答應你，你現在可以出家了吧！」

窺基沒辦法，就很勉強出家了。所以出家那天，後面有一車的酒、一車新鮮的肉、一車美女，陪著他一起到大興善寺出家（編按：大興善寺是玄奘法師的譯經場）。廟裏知道窺基要來出家，所以敲鐘擊鼓來迎接他，窺基一聽到鐘鼓的聲音，豁然大悟：「啊！原來我就是那個老修行，來幫助玄奘法師弘揚佛法。」於是乎把後面的三車遣回去，什麼都不要了。所以後人稱窺基為三車祖師。

玄奘法師取回的《唯識三十頌論》有十家，玄奘法師皆譯為華文，按照論中的意思，一字不減，一字不添，照原意譯出。此時窺基擔任整理論文，玄奘法師將十家之論譯完之後，窺基要求玄奘

Emperor Taizhong thought, "Alas! How can I promise him this? Yet Dharma Master Hsuan Tsang instructed me to grant all his requests." Therefore he said, "Fine! I agree to everything! Now you can leave the home-life!"

The nephew had no choice but to leave home. On the day that he went to Daxingshan Monastery to leave home[Note: This is where Dharma Master Hsuan Tsang translated the Sutras], he was followed by a cart of wine, a cart of fresh meat, and a cart of beautiful women. When the people in the monastery were told that the War Minister's nephew was going there to leave the home-life, they rang the bells and beat the drums. Hearing the sound of the bells and drums, Master Kueiji [the nephew's left-home name] suddenly had a great awakening: "Oh! So I was an old cultivator and now I've come to help Dharma Master Hsuan Tsang propagate the Buddhadharma." Thereupon he ordered the three carts to turn around and go back. He no longer wanted any of those things. Later generations dubbed him "The Three Cart Patriarch."

The *Thirty-stanza Consciousness Only Treatise* that Dharma Master Hsuan Tsang brought back with him from India contained ten divisions, which he translated in their entirety into Chinese. He faithfully followed the original intent of the treatise, and neither deleted nor added as much as a single word as he translated it.

Master Kueiji was in charge of the editing job, and after all ten divisions of the treatise had been fully translated by Dharma Master Hsuan Tsang, he made a request: "These ten divisions of the text all contain their strengths and weaknesses. If they fail to agree, it will certainly bring confusion and consternation to those who investigate Consciousness Only in the present and future. It might be better if we edit out the dross and keep the essentials, making just a single

法師：「這十家的論，各有其長，各有其異，若不統一，令今後學者，有歧路亡羊之苦惱，不如去其糟粕，留其精華，合成一本，令今後研究唯識的人，獲得同一的結論，不用浪費時間，而能得到法要。」玄奘法師同意他的見解是正確的，所以合成一本唯識論，即是現在的《三十頌唯識論》。玄奘法師又傳授窺基「因明學」，後來他成爲唯識專家，以宣揚唯識思想爲宗旨，成爲當代大德，爲「唯識宗」第二祖。

玄奘法師回國第二年，奉詔撰《大唐西域記》一十二卷。唐顯慶五年（西元六六〇年），玄奘法師五十九歲時，開始譯《大般若經》。《大般若經》梵本有二十萬頌，玄奘法師廣譯，不敢刪略，一如梵本，經過四年的時間，譯成六百卷。次年，擬譯《大寶積經》，不幸患病而輟筆。

唐麟德元年（西元六六四年）二月，玄奘法師圓寂，年六十有四，葬於樊川北原。玄奘法師所譯的經典有七十五部，一千三百三十五卷，成爲中國四大譯經家之一。其弟子甚多，以窺基、圓測傳承唯識，普光、神泰傳承俱舍。

volume, so that future students of Consciousness Only will be able to come to the same conclusion. In this way they will not waste time in getting to the essentials of the Dharma."

Dharma Master Hsuan Tsang agreed with his suggestion and produced the present version of the *Thirty-stanza Consciousness Only Treatise*. He later transmitted the Logic School teachings to Master Kueiji, who became an expert in Consciousness Only and made it his aim to propagate the doctrines of that school. Master Kueiji became an eminently virtuous monk of his time and was the Second Patriarch of the Consciousness Only School.

Two years after his return to China, Dharma Master Hsuan Tsang accepted an imperial appointment to compile a twelve-roll work called the *Great Tang Dynasty's Record of the Western Lands*. At age 59, in the fifth year of the Tang Dynasty's Xianqing reign-period (A.D. 660), he began to translate the *Great Prajna Sutra*. The original Sanskrit version contained 200,000 stanzas. Dharma Master Hsuan Tsang translated them entirely, not daring to omit any part of the text. He relied faithfully on the Sanskrit version, and finished the translation of 600 rolls in four years. The following year, he planned to translate the *Great Collection of Jewels Sutra*, but unfortunately had to stop working because of illness.

Dharma Master Hsuan Tsang entered Nirvana at age 64, in the second month of the first year of the Tang Dynasty's Lingde reign-period (A.D. 664). He was buried at Beiyuan (Northern Plain) near the Fan River. He had translated 75 Sutras, totalling 1,335 rolls, and thus qualified as one of China's four greatest translators of Sutras. His disciples were numerous, including Masters Kueiji and Yuance, who continued the transmission of the Consciousness Only School, and Masters Puguang and Shentai, who taught the Kosa Sect.

隋唐二朝，是佛教黃金時代，百家爭鳴，祖師輩
出，各創宗派，當時有十宗，小乘有二宗，大乘
有八宗。其中「三論宗」和「唯識宗」，完全保
存天竺原有的思想，原封不動，搬到中國來。另
外「天臺宗」（以《法華經》爲宗）和「賢首宗
」（以《華嚴經》爲宗）的思想就加入了中國的
思想，這四宗是研究佛理的，成爲教門。乃至後
來中國演變出五大宗派：教、禪、淨、律、密，
這些宗派其實目的都是同入究竟涅槃，不過修持
方法有所不同而已。

一九八〇年禪七 十二月開示

慈恩唐三藏玄奘法師

Tripitaka Dharma Master Hsuan Tsang of
the Ci En School of the Tang Dynasty

During the Tang and Sui dynasties, known as China's Golden Age of Buddhism, many schools flourished. Patriarchs appeared in succession, each establishing different sects. The foremost among those at the time were ten schools, two of which were Small Vehicle (Theravada), and eight of which were Great Vehicle (Mahayana). Two of these schools, the Three Treatise School and the Consciousness Only School, preserved in its original purity the teachings and traditional thought of Indian Buddhism and transplanted them intact into Chinese soil. Of the rest, the Tiantai School, which centered around the *Dharma Flower Sutra*, and the Xianshou (Worthy Leader) School, which centered around the *Flower Adornment Sutra*, incorporated elements of traditional Chinese thinking in their teachings. These four schools specifically investigated the principles of Buddhism, and together formed the Teachings School. Buddhism as a whole evolved into the present Five Schools: the Teachings School, the Chan Meditation School, the Pure Land School, the Vinaya School, and the Secret School. Although their actual purpose is to take us to ultimate Nirvana, the methods used are slightly different.

A talk given during a Chan Session in December, 1980

參禪要迴光返照

要迴光返照，認清自己的過錯，痛改前非，不要緊抱著臭習氣而放不下。

> 行住坐臥，不離這個；
> 離了這個，便是錯過。

「這個」是什麼？就是用功參悟的話頭。用真心來辦道，提起綿綿密密不斷的話頭來參悟，來研究。一時一刻，一分一秒，也不生雜念妄想，總是念茲在茲去參悟自己的話頭，哪有時間講話、打閒岔？也沒有時間躲懶偷安，更沒有時間說人家的是非，只是專一其心在參悟話頭。所謂：

> 事事都好去，脾氣難化了，
> 真能不生氣，就得無價寶。
> 再要不恨人，事事都能好，
> 煩惱永不生，冤孽從哪找？
> 常瞅人不對，自己苦沒了！

To Investigate Chan, We Must Look Within Ourselves

We must look within ourselves and clearly see our own faults. Then we need to earnestly repent of these past mistakes. We must not hold onto our stinking habits and fail to let them go.

A verse goes,

> *While walking, standing, sitting, and reclining,*
> *Never stray from "this."*
> *Once you stray from "this,"*
> *You've gone amiss.*

What does "this" refer to? It's talking about the meditation-topic that we work at in our investigation. We use a true mind to practice the Way. Constantly and ceaselessly, we look into the topic and investigate it. In each successive hour, minute, and second, we allow no scattered or idle thoughts to occur. In thought after thought, we only investigate our meditation topic. Who has time left over to casually talk, or to disturb others? Even less are we at leisure to take a break, or gossip about people. We simply concentrate our minds and investigate the meditation topic, seeking understanding. There is a verse that reads,

> *Things pass by quite easily,*
> *But a bad temper's truly hard to change.*
> *If you can never get angry,*
> *You've got a pearl beyond price.*
> *Then, if you can never know hatred,*

參禪打坐，具有這種思想，才能入門。在禪堂裏，每個人都要迴光返照，反求諸己，問問自己，是在用功？還是在打妄想？看看自己，是迴光返照照自己？還是反光鏡照外邊？這一點要特別注意。

在禪堂裏，要記住這兩句話：

> 摩訶薩不管他，
> 彌陀佛各顧各。

時時刻刻管自己，不要去管他人。更不可打閒岔，障礙人家用功修道，耽誤他人開悟的時光，這種行為最要不得。我常對你們說：

> 真認自己錯，
> 莫論他人非；
> 他非即我非，
> 同體名大悲。

人人有這種思想，就會一心一意用功辦道，並無二想，不會亂講話、打閒岔。

24

Everything will go your way.
Since afflictions never bother you anymore,
Your evil karma no longer comes to call.
But someone who knows only to criticize others
Is one whose own suffering has not yet ended.

Only if you maintain these attitudes as you meditate, do you have hope of "entering the gate." People in the Chan Hall must reflect inwardly and seek within themselves. Introspect and ask, "Am I working hard, or am I engaging in idle thoughts?" Take a close look at yourself: are you reflecting the light inwardly, or shining it out to mirror the exterior surroundings? Pay especially close attention to this question.

Remember this statement as you work in the Chan Hall:

Mahasattvas pay no attention to others;
Amitabha! Every man for himself!

At all times watch over yourself, and don't supervise others. Even less should you disturb others, obstructing them from diligently cultivating the Way and denying them their chance to get enlightened. Such behavior is most despicable. As I often say to you all:

Truly recognize your own faults,
And don't discuss the faults of others.
Others' faults are simply my own faults:
Being one in substance with all is called Great Compassion.

If we can all think this way, then everyone will work hard, with single-minded concentration. No one will have any interest in idle chatter or disturbing others.

參禪的人，要把根本問題認識清楚，什麼問題？就是習氣毛病。我們打禪七，就是打掉惡習氣、壞毛病，洗心滌慮，解除妒賢嫉能的心理。把嫉妒障礙心、無明煩惱心，統統滅盡，這樣真心現出，智慧現前，才有好消息。

人為什麼講是講非？因為愚癡。為什麼嫉妒障礙？因為愚癡。為什麼有害人心？因為愚癡。凡是做出不合理的事，都因為愚癡。為什麼愚癡？因為沒有禪定的功夫，所以沒有智慧，在人我是非圈中轉，跳不出圈外。對於這一點，我們要迴光返照，認清自己的過錯，痛改前非，不要緊抱著臭習氣而放不下。

打坐的時候，為什麼要睡覺？因為求法心不真實；如果真心求道，絕對不會睡覺。大家不妨試一試這個道理正確不正確？

一九八〇年禪七 十二月開示

People who practice Chan meditation should be clear about the basic problem. What is the basic problem? It is our bad habits and faults. When we attend a Chan meditation session, we aim to eliminate those bad habits and faults. Wash the mind clean and purify your thoughts. Purge yourself of jealousy towards worthy and capable individuals. Banish forever all thoughts of envy and obstructiveness, of ignorance and afflictions. If you can do this, then your true mind, your wisdom, will manifest, and then there will be good news.

Why would people gossip? Only due to their stupidity. Why would they indulge in envy and obstructiveness? Because of stupidity. Why would they want to harm others? Because of stupidity. In fact, we do all sorts of unreasonable things because of our stupidity. Why are we stupid? It's because we lack the skills of Chan samadhi, and so we have no wisdom. We turn forever in the little sphere of self and others, rights and wrongs, and can't find our way out of that tight circle. This is the place where we must look within ourselves and clearly see our own faults. Then we need to earnestly repent of these past mistakes. We must not hold onto our stinking habits and fail to let them go.

Why do we fall asleep when we should be meditating? It's because we aren't sincere in seeking the Dharma. Someone who is sincere in seeking the Dharma would definitely not fall asleep. Why don't you all check this principle out and see if it is correct?

Chan Session Instruction in December, 1980

禪堂是選佛的道場

你若是總戴著假面具，
是不會被選爲佛的。

大家在禪堂裏，參禪打坐，就是考試，看誰能考
上佛的果位？怎樣才能考上呢？就要內無身心，
外無世界，所謂：

> 視之不見，
> 聽之不聞，
> 嗅之無味。

有了這種功夫，才有被錄取的希望。

爲什麼說：視之不見？因爲迴光返照。爲什麼說
：聽之不聞？因爲反聞聞自性。爲什麼說：嗅之
無味？因爲收攝身心，不爲味塵所轉。這時，眼
觀色而無色，耳聽聲而無聲，鼻嗅香而無香，舌
嚐味而無味，身覺觸而不著觸，意知法而不著法
。到了這種境界，才有被選爲佛的希望。不到爐

The Meditation Hall Is a Way-place Where Buddhas Are Selected

If you always wear a phony mask to cover yourself, you'll never get selected to be a Buddha.

People who meditate in the Chan Hall are actually taking a test. They are seeing whether or not they qualify for Buddhahood. How can they pass this test? Reach the state where, "Inside there is no body or mind, and outside there is no world."

It's a state of:

> *Looking, but not seeing;*
> *Hearing, but not listening;*
> *Smelling, but not noticing the scent.*

Only a person who possesses this kind of skill can hope to pass the test.

Why is it described as "looking, but not seeing"? Because the person is "returning the light to shine within," and introspecting. Why is it "hearing, but not listening"? Because he is "turning the hearing back to listen to his own nature." Why does it say, "smelling, but not noticing the scent"? Because he has gathered back his body and mind, and is not disturbed any longer by scents. At this time, the cultivator's eyes contemplate physical forms, but the forms don't exist for him. His ears hear sounds, but the sounds don't exist for him. His nose smells scents, but those scents don't

火純青的時候，不到登峰造極的時候，不到百尺竿頭更進一步的時候，那是沒有希望的。所以在禪堂裏，不要把寶貴的光陰空過。

古人說：

> 一寸光陰一寸金，
>
> 寸金難買寸光陰；
>
> 失落寸金容易得，
> 光陰過去難再尋。

我們要把握時機，認真用功修行。修行之法甚多，唯獨「參禪」這個法門，是最高無上的法門。這個法門，如果用功用到相當時，能回過頭來，能轉過身，背塵合覺，被選為佛。

修菩薩道的人，外能捨國城妻子，內能捨頭目腦髓，只要有人需要，他一切皆布施，絕不慳吝，他只知道利益眾生，而不為自己打算。能有這樣的思想，在選佛場中才有希望被選中。大家要知道，這是諸佛來選拔，絕對是大公無私的，沒有人可以僥倖被錄取，這完全要靠真功夫的。

exist for him. His tongue tastes flavors, but for him, those flavors don't exist. His body feels sensations, but does not attach itself to those sensations. His mind knows of things (dharmas), but does not attach to them. Only when one reaches this kind of state does one have any hope of being chosen as a Buddha. Before you reach perfection, before you reach the highest summit, before you "climb to the very top of a hundred-foot pole, and take one further step," you have no hope at all of qualifying. Therefore, don't waste your precious time here in the meditation hall.

Ancient cultivators had a proverb that goes,

An instant of time is worth more than an ounce of gold.
You can't buy an instant of time with an ounce of gold.
An ounce of gold, if lost, can be easily replaced.
But once time has gone by, you can't bring it back again.

We must make the most of our opportunity to work hard and diligently cultivate. There are many ways to cultivate, but Chan meditation is surely the most lofty and supreme Dharma-door. When your efforts in cultivating this Dharma-door reach maturity, you'll be able to turn around, so that you "turn your back on the dust and unite with enlightenment," and get selected as a Buddha.

People who cultivate the Bodhisattva Path are able to renounce their external wealth, such as their countries, cities, wives, and children. They're also able to renounce their internal wealth, such as their heads, eyes, brains, and bone marrow. Bodhisattvas are able to give people anything they need; they are never stingy. A Bodhisattva's sole concern is to aid people; he doesn't calculate on his own behalf. Only one with this kind of attitude has hope of being chosen for Buddhahood here in the "Buddha-selecting field."

佛來選佛，而不是魔來選佛，可是魔來助佛。佛是在正面教化眾生，魔在反面教化眾生，反面來鼓勵你，給你機會發大願力，用功修行。所以魔是反面的善知識，我常說：

魔是磨眞道，眞道才有魔；
越磨越光亮，光亮更要磨。
磨如空中月，空中照群魔；
群魔照化了，現出本來佛。

所以對魔不要有敵對的心理，要把他當做助道的善知識。如是觀想，便心安理得無煩惱。有人來誹謗我們，那是我們的善知識。我們本來做得對，可是有人批評我們不對，那麼就要往對的更進一步去做，所謂「百尺竿頭，更進一步。」「見吾過者是吾師」，能說出我們毛病的這個人，就是我們的老師，應該感謝他，不可對他仇視。

諸佛不像我們那樣糊塗，你若是總戴著假面具，是不會被選爲佛的。你要眞裏求眞，眞中更眞，要「眞眞眞眞眞眞眞！」有七個眞，才有希望被

Everyone should know that the selection is done by the Buddhas, and they are completely unbiased and impartial. No one can hope to attain Buddhahood by chance or luck. The only criterion is true spiritual skill.

Buddhas select other Buddhas; demons don't select Buddhas. Demons, however, do help Buddhas. Buddhas teach living beings in a direct manner, while demons teach living beings indirectly, from the reverse side of things. From the flip-side they exhort you on, giving you a chance to bring forth great resolutions and to apply yourself to serious cultivation. Demons thus count as Good and Wise Advisors in an indirect way.

I've often said:

> *Demons polish the True Way.*
> *Only when the Way is true do the demons come.*
> *The more they polish, the brighter you get.*
> *The brighter you get, the more they polish you;*
> *Polishing until you shine like the moon in space,*
> *Which glows in the sky and*
> *Sheds light on the hordes of demons.*
> *When those hordes retreat before your light*
> *Your fundamental Buddha-nature appears.*

We needn't see demons as our adversaries. Treat them, rather, as our Good and Wise Advisors who aid us along the Way. If you can contemplate them from this viewpoint, then your mind will rest calm, and you'll be free of afflictions. People who slander us are really our Good and Wise Advisors. When we've performed correctly, but somebody finds fault with our job, then we should strive to further improve, and take one more step from atop the hundred-foot pole. "The person who finds my faults I will treat as

選拔。所謂「七眞八正」，在禪七中，七天要眞
修行，第八天就改邪歸正。這時，所有的習氣毛
病都一掃而光，脫落淨盡了！

一九八〇年禪七 十二月開示

my teacher." An individual who can point out our shortcomings is our teacher. We ought to show him gratitude and never feel antagonism or hostility towards him.

Buddhas would never be as muddled as we common people. If you always wear a phony mask to cover yourself, you'll never get selected to be a Buddha. You must be true within true, and truer than true. You have to be *true, true, true, true, true, true, true!* Seven times true! Then you can qualify. This is to be "seven times true and eight times correct" [an expression which means one must be thoroughly genuine and proper]. During the seven days of the Chan session, you genuinely cultivate, and on the eighth day you straighten out any crooked views. All bad habits and faults get swept away completely, and you are flawlessly pure, to the ultimate!

A talk given during a Chan Session in December, 1980

什麼是無心道人？

修道要憑眞功夫，不要自我宣傳。

在《四十二章經》上說：供養十方三世諸佛，不如供養一個無心道人。什麼是無心道人？就是在禪堂打禪七的人。他們沒有求名求利的心，他們把財色名食睡地獄五條根，都拔出來，無心無念地在參禪，所以叫無心道人。

在西方想要眞正弘揚佛法，就要修「無心道人」的法門。說這個，並不是希望有人來護法供養無心道人；如果貪圖供養，那就是有心。所以我們在打坐的時候，要老老實實參禪習定，不可以妄想叢生，接二連三，像演電影一般，一幕一幕現在眼前，那就離道有十萬八千里了。你越走離家越遠，成爲一個外鄉的遊子，這是多麼可憐啊！

我們修道，要躬行實踐，憑眞功夫。不要搞名搞

What Is a "Person of the Way Who Is Without Thoughts"?

In cultivating the Way, actual skill is all that counts. Don't publicize yourself.

"Making offerings to all Buddhas of the ten directions and the three periods of time is not as good as making offerings to a single person of the Way who is without thoughts." What is a "person of the Way who is without thoughts"? This refers to anyone who is taking part in the Chan Session here in the meditation hall. These people have no thoughts of seeking fame and benefit, for they have already eradicated the five roots of the hells: wealth, sex, fame, food, and sleep. Because they are free of thoughts as they investigate Chan, they are called people of the Way who are without thoughts.

Here in the West, a person who truly wants to propagate the Buddhadharma must cultivate the Dharma-door of a "person of the Way who is without thoughts." In saying this, it's not that we're hoping somebody will come to protect or make offerings to these people of the Way who are without thoughts. If we craved offerings, we would not be free of thoughts. Therefore, as we meditate, we should honestly investigate Chan and cultivate our concentration. We must not let our idle thoughts arise in profusion, one after another, like a movie flashing scene after scene on the screen before our eyes. To do so is to leave the Way a million miles behind. The farther we run, the farther we are from home. We wind up like the prodigal son wandering in a foreign land. How pitiful!

利，不要自我宣傳。要學文殊、普賢、觀世音、地藏王諸大菩薩的精神，護持道場，教化眾生。菩薩認為眾生有成就和自己有成就是一樣的，他們沒有你我的分別，菩薩是見聞隨喜，來讚歎有功德的人。

俗語說：「有麝自然香，何須大風揚？」無心道人修到極點，自然有感應。做佛事就是佛，做菩薩事就是菩薩，做羅漢事就是羅漢，做鬼事就是鬼，這是很自然的現象。修道不可以找捷徑，投機取巧。要腳踏實地，按部就班，認真去修行，才能有所成就。

一九八〇年禪七 十二月開示

People who cultivate the Way want to really do the work with effort; actual skill is all that counts. Don't crave fame and profits; don't publicize yourself. Follow the spirit of the Bodhisattvas Manjushri, Samantabhadra (Universal Worthy), Avalokiteshvara (Guanshiyin), and Ksitigarbha (Earth Treasury) as they guard the Way-place and teach and transform living beings. These Bodhisattvas feel that living beings' accomplishments are the same as their own accomplishment. They don't make distinctions between self and others. Bodhisattvas joyfully support the merit and virtue they see and hear others doing.

There's a saying,

> When the musk deer arrives,
> We will naturally know because of its scent.
> There is no need for fanfare.

When people of the Way who are without thoughts cultivate to the ultimate point, they naturally gain a response to their efforts. When one does what Buddhas do, one is a Buddha. When one does what Bodhisattvas do, one is a Bodhisattva. When one does what Arhats do, one is an Arhat. When one does what ghosts do, one is a ghost. These are all natural phenomena. There are no shortcuts in cultivation. You cannot cut corners and hedge bets. Success comes only after one does an honest job, proceeding step-by-step, sincerely and truly cultivating the Way.

A talk given during a Chan Session in December, 1980

參禪是行六度波羅蜜

緊了繃，慢了鬆，不緊不慢才成功。

做維那要注意，在開靜的時候，先打一下引磬，令大家準備站起來；看看大家準備妥當，再打第二下引磬。這時，大家一起站起來，然後再打兩聲木魚，大家就開始行起來。在跑香的時候，分爲內外兩圈，跑快的人在外圈跑，跑慢的人在內圈跑，這是折衷的辦法。大家自在來修行，快慢均可，所謂「緊了繃，慢了鬆，不緊不慢才成功。」這是沒有定法。

在《金剛經》上説：「無有定法。名阿耨多羅三藐三菩提。」要是説一定，就會發生毛病。

《金剛經》又説：「是法平等。無有高下。」修行這個法，都要平等。佛雖然有三身、四智、五眼、六通，可是佛不覺得和眾生有什麼不同，所

Chan Meditation Involves Practicing the Six Paramitas

Haste will make you stumble; tarry, and you'll fall behind. Not too fast, and not too slow, you'll get there right on time.

Each of you who has the job of Ceremony Master, please note that when the meditation period is over, you should hit the handbell once to alert the sitters that it is time to stand up. When you see that they are all ready to stand, hit the bell again. At that signal, everyone will stand up together. The Ceremony Master then will strike the wooden fish two times to signal the beginning of the walking meditation period. During the walk, we should make two separate lanes: one for fast walkers, and one for slower walkers. The faster walkers should use the outer lane, and the slower walkers should use the inner lane. This is a way to ensure harmony, so that everybody can be free and at ease in their cultivation. Both slow and fast walkers are accommodated. A saying goes,

> *Haste will make you stumble;*
> *Tarry, and you'll fall behind.*
> *Not too fast, and not too slow,*
> *You'll get there right on time.*

This is the principle of there being no fixed dharmas. A line from the *Vajra Sutra (Diamond Sutra)* says, "There is no fixed dharma known as Unsurpassed, Proper, Equal, and Right Enlightenment (Anuttara-samyaksambodhi)." As soon as you want to determine a dharma absolutely, you'll create a problem right there.

謂「心、佛、眾生，三無差別。」心是佛，佛是眾生；眾生是佛，佛是心。

走得快也是參禪，走得慢也是參禪，隨自己的體力來決定。要任運自然，一點也不造作，一點也不要勉強，要這樣精進、用功、忍耐。腰痠腿痛，不要管它。什麼也不要了，這就是布施。身不去做惡，這是身業清淨；口不說是非，這是口業清淨；心不打妄想，這是意業清淨。三業清淨，就是持戒。能忍受一切痛苦，就是忍辱。能不斷地用功修道，無論遇到什麼困難，都不退心，就是精進。能坐下來，如如不動，了了常明，就是禪定。由禪定而生智慧，就是般若。六度圓滿，便到彼岸。

到止靜的時候，維那要看班首已經到了他的座位前，便敲一下木魚。每個人各自站在自己的座位前，等大家都站齊，再敲一下木魚，這時，要端然正坐，把脊背挺直，不可低頭彎腰，所謂「坐如鐘」，頭要正，腰要直，好像一個大鐘，四平八穩的。

Another line from the *Vajra Sutra* says, "The Dharma is equal and impartial; it has no aspects higher or lower than any other." Therefore, as we cultivate the Dharma, we want to be impartial. Even though the Buddha possesses the Three Bodies, Four Modes of Wisdom, Five Spiritual Eyes, and Six Wisdom Powers, he does not feel that he is in any way different from living beings. As it's said, "The mind, the Buddha, and living beings are one and the same, and are in no way distinguishable from one another." The mind is the Buddha, and the Buddha is living beings; living beings are the Buddha, and the Buddha is the mind.

You can investigate Chan while walking quickly; you can also investigate Chan while walking slowly. Set your own pace according to your own physical strength. Let your walking speed be completely natural; don't be artificial in the least. Avoid forcing it; just be vigorous as you work, and be patient. Even if your back hurts or your legs ache, pay them no mind. You should want nothing; just that is giving. When the body doesn't do anything bad, this is purity in physical karma. When the mouth doesn't say evil things, this is purity in speech karma. When the mind doesn't indulge in idle thoughts, this is purity in mental karma. When these three modes of karma are purified, then you are upholding precepts. If you can endure any kind of pain, then this is patience. If you can apply yourself without cease to the cultivation of the Way, if you never retreat regardless of the difficulties you encounter, then this is vigor. If you can sit down and become "Thus, thus unmoving, resolved, and always clear," then this is Chan samadhi. Wisdom is born of Chan samadhi, and this wisdom is Prajna. When these Six Paramitas are perfected, you can reach the other shore.

When it's time to end the walk, the Ceremony Master watches for the senior monk to return to his seat, then he strikes the wooden fish

43

參「念佛是誰？」不是念這句話，而是參這句話，研究這個「誰」字。有人說：「我知道，念佛是我。」這是不對的。這句話頭，若是明白了，就是明心見性，徹法底源，借道還家。不是像你所說那麼樣地簡單，那樣地容易，「就是我嘛！我在念佛。」你在念佛？那麼人死了之後，還有人在念佛嗎？說：「沒有了。」既然沒有，怎麼會是你在念佛？要曉得念佛的人是不會死的，你會死，那念佛的不是你。念佛成佛，成佛的又是誰？誰去成佛？你已經死了。所以就在這個地方要參，參到海枯石爛，也不放鬆，追根究底地參，終會有水落石出的一天——豁然大悟，原來如此！

一九八〇年禪七 十二月開示

once. When everyone has returned to his seat, the Ceremony Master strikes it once more, and everyone sits upright and properly with a straight back, without letting the head droop or the back curve. This is called "sitting like a bell." This means the head is erect and the back is straight, just like a great iron bell, very stable and solid.

Investigate the sentence: "Who is reciting the Buddha's name?" Don't merely recite the sentence, but investigate it, look into the word "who." Someone may say, "I know, the one reciting the Buddha's name is me!" That's wrong. If you really understand the answer to this meditation topic, then you can "understand your mind and see your nature." Then you have "penetrated to the the source of Dharma," and you have "found your way home." To understand is not as simple a matter as you make it out to be. "It's just me! I'm the reciter!" you insist. Well, after you die, is there anyone still reciting? No, there isn't. Since there isn't, how can you claim that you are there reciting the Buddha's name? You should realize that the person who recites the Buddha's name is a person who does not die. You, however, can die, so you can't be considered the one who is reciting. We recite the Buddha's name, and we can become Buddhas. But who is the one who becomes a Buddha? Who goes realizes Buddhahood? You've already died. This is what you must look into, and don't slack off even when "the ocean dries up and solid rocks fall apart." Investigate to the ultimate point; then you'll see the waters part and the rocks appear. Suddenly you'll enlighten to the truth that it was just this way all along!

A talk given during a Chan Session in December, 1980

45

要修無相的功德

把妄心停下來，現出真心來修道，
就有無量功德。

在禪堂裏是選佛的地方，是種功德福田的地方，
所謂：

> 若人靜坐一須臾，
> 勝造恆沙七寶塔。

為什麼要這樣說呢？因為在外邊所造的塔寺，是
有形有相的功德。

在《金剛經》上說：

> 凡所有相。皆是虛妄。
> 若見諸相非相。即見如來。

若能靜坐片刻的時間，就有永不磨滅的功德。有
人說：「那外邊的功德我不做了，我來修內邊的
功德。」這種思想也是不對的。我們兩種都要做

Cultivate Merit and Virtue without Marks

If you can stop your idle thoughts and cultivate the Way with your true mind, then your merit and virtue will be measureless and boundless.

The Chan Hall is a place where Buddhas are selected; it's a field where we plant blessings, merit, and virtue. As the saying goes,

> *If a person can sit in stillness for even an instant,*
> *His merit surpasses that of someone who builds as many stupas*
> *of the seven treasures as there are sand grains in the Ganges.*

Why is this so? Because temples and stupas that are built outside are visible forms of merit and virtue.

The *Vajra Sutra* has a line that goes,

> *All appearances are false and unreal.*
> *If one sees all appearances as no appearances,*
> *then one sees the Tathagata.*

If a person can sit in stillness for the briefest time, he creates merit and virtue which will never disappear. At this, someone may say, "I won't create any more external merit and virtue; I'm going to have only inner merit and virtue from now on." It's also wrong to think that way. In fact, you must cultivate both kinds of merit and virtue. When your merit and virtue are perfected and your blessings and wisdom are complete, you will be known as the Doubly-Perfected Honored One.

，既要修功，又要修德，到功德圓滿的時候，福慧具足，就是兩足尊了。

當知外邊所造的寺廟，經過長時間，都會變壞；所建的塔，經過劫火，也會被燒空的。唯獨靜坐能把自性中的佛法僧三寶修行成功，這是無漏的功德，不怕風雨，不怕劫火，永遠存在，所以無相功德勝於有相功德千萬倍。

在禪堂裏，把妄心停下來，現出眞心來修道，就有無量功德，否則就無功德。所以才說：「你能靜坐片刻的時間，就勝過造恆河沙數那樣多的七寶塔，比那功德還要大。」

各位來參加打禪七，都是有善根，才遇到這種因緣，共同來參禪。現在要把心清淨下來，不可心猿意馬，時刻不安靜，總想向外跑。那就與道不相應，浪費了七天的光陰，一無所得，辜負當初的發心。要設法控制妄念，令心靜下來，所謂：

　　　　心清水現月，
　　　　意定天無雲。

Know, too, that any temple you can build outside will surely decay over time. Any stupa that you can erect will be burned to ashes when the fires blaze at the end of the eon. Only through Chan meditation can you successfully cultivate the Triple Jewel—the Buddha, Dharma, and Sangha—of your own nature. The merit and virtue of this cultivation is "merit and virtue free of outflows." It is not endangered by the wind, the floods or fires at the eon's end, or by anything else. This is merit and virtue that lasts forever. So this kind of invisible merit and virtue surpasses visible merit and virtue by a million times over.

Here in the Chan Hall, if you can stop your idle thoughts and cultivate the Way with your true mind, then your merit and virtue will be measureless and boundless. But if you cannot do this, you'll have no merit and virtue to speak of. And so the saying goes, "If a person can sit in stillness for even an instant, his merit surpasses that of someone who builds as many stupas of the seven treasures as there are sand grains in the Ganges."

All of us who have come to take part in this Chan Session have good roots. That's why we have the chance to come together to investigate Chan. Now we must make our minds clear and calm, and not let our thoughts run outside like mad monkeys or wild horses, or else we won't get even a moment of stillness. Then we won't have any response in the Way, and we'll have wasted seven days of time. We won't gain anything, and we will have failed to achieve what we initially resolved to do. So we must come up with a method to control our idle thoughts and settle our minds. It is said,

When the heart is pure, the moon appears in the water.
When the mind is in samadhi, then there are no clouds in the sky.

49

因爲這種原因，我們明年（一九八二年）準備舉行十個禪七，靜坐七十天。今時今日，在全世界可以說找不到連續打十個禪七的道場了。

萬佛聖城要將末法改變爲正法，所以我們拼命修行，用功辦道。如果有人想實實在在修行，只有到萬佛聖城來，才有機會眞正修行。在外邊修行，不過在皮毛上打轉，敷衍了事。名義上說是打禪七，實際上時間有所不同。萬佛聖城打禪七，從早上二點半鐘開始行香，到夜裏十二點才休息，中間只有一小時的養息香，這是我們打禪七的規矩。

一九八〇年禪七 十二月開示

For this reason we've already decided that next year (1982) we'll convene a ten-week Chan Session and sit in meditation for seventy days. In this day and age, I believe you won't find another Way-place anywhere in the world that holds ten consecutive weeks of Chan meditation.

Our goal at the City of Ten Thousand Buddhas is to turn the Dharma-ending Age into the Proper Dharma Age. That's why we cultivate as if our lives depended on it; that's why we work hard at cultivating the Way. If you truly want to cultivate the Way, you'll have the opportunity to do so only at the City of Ten Thousand Buddhas. At most other places, the cultivation is pretty superficial; they just go through the motions. Perhaps they say they're holding a Chan Session, but their schedules are quite different. At the City of Ten Thousand Buddhas, the daily schedule of meditation during the Chan Sessions begins with walking meditation at 2:30 in the morning and continues without pause until midnight. In between, there's only one hour when we are not meditating. This is the rule at our Chan Sessions.

A talk given during a Chan Session in December, 1980

虛雲老和尚出家的因緣

志不退，願不退，行不退，
一心一意向前精進。

虛老是湖南省湘鄉人氏，俗姓蕭，父玉堂公，
曾任福建省泉州府知府之職，爲官清廉，愛民
如子。年逾四十，膝下無子，夫婦到城外觀音
古寺求子。心誠則有感應，回府之後，夫人果
然懷孕。十月期滿，夫婦同夢一位老者，長鬚
青袍，頭頂觀音，跨虎而來。驚醒，胎兒降生
，乃是一肉團（八地菩薩，才有此境界），母
驚嚇而氣絕。

翌日，來了一位賣藥的老翁，用刀將肉團剖開
，內裏有一男嬰，遂由庶母撫育。虛老因爲有
善根，不歡喜讀儒家的書籍，對功名視爲浮雲
，可是對佛經頗有興趣，所以在年少就萌起出
家修道的念頭。有一次，逃到福州鼓山擬出家
，被家人找回。其父遣之回湖南老家去，請二

The Story of Venerable Master Hsu Yun's Leaving the Home-life

Never retreat from your resolve, from your vows, and from your practice. Advance with single-minded vigor.

The Venerable Master Hsu Yun (Empty Cloud) was born to the Xiao family and was a native of Xiang County of Hunan Province in China. His father, the Elder Yutang, was an incorruptible magistrate of Quan Prefecture in Fujian province who loved the people as if they were his own children. At the age of forty, he was still childless. One day, he and his wife went to the ancient Guanyin Temple outside of town to pray for a son. Their sincerity inspired a response; soon after their return to the prefecture, Mrs. Xiao conceived a child. When the pregnancy reached full term, one night both husband and wife dreamed of a long-bearded old man, wearing a dark-green robe and bearing an image of Guanyin Bodhisattva on his head, who came riding astride a tiger. Startled awake, the woman delivered a child who emerged in a bag of flesh. (This is the state of Bodhisattvas at the eighth stage or above). Frightened by the uncanny event, the woman passed away.

The following day an old peddler of medicines passed by and cut open the flesh-bag to reveal a baby boy inside. The child was raised by his stepmother. Endowed with keen faculties, the boy considered honor and position to be meaningless. Rather than delighting in the Confucian classics, he had a consuming interest in studying the Buddhist Sutras, and at an early age, he conceived the idea of leaving the home-life to cultivate the Way. Once, he tried escaping

叔嚴加管教，杜絕其出家之念。

虛老是獨生子，三叔很早就往生，沒有兒子，所以就成為「一支兩不絕」的繼承人。按照當時的風俗，可以娶兩個太太，一個是父母的媳婦，一個是叔父的媳婦，使兩支都有後代，可以延續香煙。這是一舉兩得的事，一般人求之不得，可是虛老認為是苦惱事。

為傳宗接代的使命，奉父叔之命，在十八歲時，和田氏、譚氏二女，同時舉行結婚儀式。這二女都是名門閨秀，深明大義。結婚之夜，虛老向二女約法三章，有夫妻之名，無夫妻之實，保持童真之體，三人同居，互不侵犯，相安無事。

次年，虛老決心出家修道，徵求二女同意（此二女後來亦出家為尼），偷偷離開溫暖的家，來到福州鼓山湧泉寺，禮妙蓮長老為師，名演徹，號德清。虛老深恐被家人再找到，所以在

to Gu Mountain in Fu Prefecture to become a monk, but his family dragged him back home. His father ordered him to return to their old home in Hunan, and told his uncle to keep a close watch over him and to drive the idea of leaving home out of his mind.

The Venerable Master Hsu Yun was the only child in the family. His third uncle had passed away long ago, leaving no descendants. Thus he became the heir of two branches of the family. By social custom, he was entitled to marry two wives; one to be the daughter-in-law of his parents, and the other to be the daughter-in-law of his uncle. In this way, both branches could have heirs, and both family lines could continue. To get "two birds with one stone" was a situation most men might seek but never find, but to Venerable Master Hsu Yun, it only meant suffering and affliction.

In order to preserve the family lineage, he obeyed his father and uncle, and, at age eighteen, he married Miss Tan and Miss Tian in a double wedding. Both women were well-bred daughters of noble families, and both had deep understanding of ethical conduct. On the night of their wedding, the Venerable Master Hsu Yun entered into a solemn oath with the two young women, promising that their marriage was to be in name only, and that they would never consummate their troth. Maintaining their virginity, the three of them lived together without sharing husband-wife relations.

The following year, the Venerable Master decided to leave the home-life and cultivate the Way. But first he obtained the permission of his two wives, who later both left home to become nuns. He then secretly stole away from his comfortable home and travelled to Yongquan ("Bubbling Spring") Monastery on Gu Mountain in Fu Prefecture to become the disciple of Elder Master

深山巖下修苦行，飢時吃松子和草葉，渴時喝
山澗之溪水。這種苦行，不是一般人所能修持
的，所謂：

> 穿人所不能穿，
> 吃人所不能吃，
> 忍人所不能忍，
> 受人所不能受。

面臨種種考驗，他卻受之泰然，不但不覺得痛
苦，反而感覺快樂。

三年之後，他爲了親近善知識，爲了研究佛法
，於是到處參方。他跋山涉水，歷盡艱辛，凡
有高僧大德所在之處，無論是千山萬水，也擋
不住他求道爲法的心。在參方期間，處處受到
歧視，可是虛老本著堅忍不拔的意志，爲求法
而忘己，雖然經過多次的挫折，也不灰心，不
變初衷，依然勇猛向前，精進學習。虛老這種
精神，實在令人欽佩，足以爲人效法。

Miaolian ("Wonderful Lotus"), who gave him the names Yence ("Thorough Expression"), and Deqing ("Virtuous and Pure"). Fearing that his family might find him again, Venerable Master Hsu Yun went off to the remote mountain wilds to live as an ascetic. When hungry, he ate pine nuts and wild plants; when thirsty, he drank mountain spring water. The bitter conditions were certainly beyond the tolerance of ordinary people, but he was one who could:

> *Wear what others cannot wear;*
> *Eat what others cannot eat;*
> *Endure what others cannot endure; and,*
> *Tolerate what others cannot tolerate.*

He faced numerous tests, but he passed each one with a peaceful, tolerant attitude. Instead of feeling miserable, he felt very happy.

Three years later, in order to draw near to good and wise advisors and to investigate the Buddhadharma, he embarked on a study-tour. Crossing mountains and fording streams, he suffered untold hardships. As long as it was a place where eminent, virtuous monks resided, all the mountains and rivers couldn't impede him from going there to seek the Way and dedicate himself to the Dharma. He met prejudice and troubles at every turn of the road, but he stood firm in his indefatigable resolve and simply forgot himself in his quest for the Dharma. Despite continual setbacks, he never gave up, nor lost sight of his initial purpose. Instead, he simply forged ahead and studied with even more vigor. This spirit inspired others' respect and caused many people to emulate him.

Later on, he made a vow to undertake a pilgrimage in which he would bow to the ground once every three steps, in order to repay the kindness of his mother. His route took him from Potala Mountain to Five Peaks Mountain, and he made prostrations all the

後來爲報母恩，他發心三步一拜，從普陀山拜
向五臺山。經過三年的時間，完成志願，功德
圓滿。以下敘述虛老在三步一拜時，所發生的
感應道交的小故事。

虛老拜到黃河岸的時候，正逢天降大雪，三天
三夜下得不停。他住在小草棚中，又飢又寒，
已經失去身體的知覺，不省人事。醒來時，發
現有一個乞丐爲他做飯，他吃了之後，恢復元
氣，於是繼續朝拜五臺山。後來到五臺山，才
知道這個乞丐原來是文殊菩薩的化身。

虛老在九華山住茅棚的時候，聽說揚州高旻寺
打八個禪七，就想去參加。他從九華山沿江而
行，當時正逢大雨季節，江水氾濫，水漫路面
，他不愼失足，掉落水中，漂流二十四小時之
久，流到采石磯附近時，被打魚的網打上來。
這個時候，虛老已經奄奄一息。漁夫通知附近
的寶積寺，將他抬回寺中，於是被救活，可是
他七孔流血，病況十分嚴重。休息數日後，他

way. Three years later he fulfilled his vow, and the merit and virtue of the pilgrimage was completed. The following is a brief account of one of the responses the Venerable Master Hsu Yun experienced in the course of his pilgrimage.

He had bowed to the banks of the Yellow River, when a huge snow-storm blew up, dropping powdery snow for three days and nights without cease. The Master stayed in a tiny hut and suffered from hunger and cold. Finally he lost consciousness and fainted. When he revived, he saw a beggar sitting nearby, fixing him food. After eating the meal, he recovered his strength and continued to bow towards Five Peaks Mountain. Upon his arrival, he discovered that the beggar had been none other than a transformation body of Manjushri Bodhisattva.

While the Elder Master Hsu Yun was living as a hermit on Jiuhua ("Nine Flowers") Mountain, news came to him that Gaomin Monastery in Yang Zhou Province was preparing to host an eight-week Chan meditation retreat, and he decided to participate. He walked down from Jiuhua Mountain, steering his course by the river-bank. It was the rainy season, and at that time the river was flooded and had overflowed its banks on the road ahead of him. Suddenly the Master lost his footing on the treacherous path and fell into the river, where he bobbed and floated for twenty-four hours. The current carried him downstream near Cai Jetty, where he was caught by a fisherman's net. By that time the Venerable Master was nearly drowned. The fisherman pulled him up, then informed the nearby temple. Monks from Baoji ("Jewel Cluster") Monastery carried the Master back to the temple, where they revived him. The Venerable Master was bleeding from seven orifices, and was in critical condition, but he would not give up his original intent. After resting for a few days, the Master set aside his personal welfare for

爲法忘軀，將生死置於度外，還是不變初衷，
仍然到高旻寺參加禪七。

高旻寺規矩非常嚴格，執行非常認眞，如果有
犯規矩的，就打香板，毫不客氣。當時住持月
朗禪師，請他代職，虛老不答應，遂按規矩打
香板。虛老接受不語，但經責打之後，他的病
勢加重，血流不止，病況危殆。

有人在想：「虛老這麼樣用功修道，爲什麼護
法神不護持？還讓他掉在水裏？」其實，還是
護法神在護持，不然的話，漁夫怎麼會用網把
他打上來？所以在冥冥之中，都有佑護。

這也是生死的考驗，看他遭受這次的災難，有
什麼感想？是不是生了退道心？「啊！我修行
這麼多年，又讀經，又拜懺，又燃指，又住茅
棚，種種的苦行，我都認眞去修，爲什麼一點
感應也沒有？算了吧！我不修行了，我要還俗

the sake of the Dharma, and, putting life and death out of his mind, he went on to Gaomin Monastery to join the Chan retreat.

According to Gaomin Monastery's extremely strict regulations and their high standards of practice, anybody who broke the rules earned a beating with the incense-board (discipline-rod); there was no recourse to courtesy at all. The acting abbot, Chan Master Yue Lang ("Moon Radiance"), had requested the Venerable Hsu Yun to substitute for him in his position as official administrator. The Venerable Master declined the request, and thereby, according to the rules of the monastery, deserved a beating. He took his punishment without complaint. But after the beating, his illness grew worse; he bled non-stop from every orifice and his condition grew nearly fatal.

Someone may be wondering, "Since Venerable Hsu Yun was a sincere and diligent cultivator, why did the Dharma-protecting spirits fail to protect him, and let him fall into the river like that?" In fact, the spirits were still protecting him. If not, then how could he have been saved in the fisherman's net? Thus, we can know that he was protected invisibly at all times by the Dharma-protecting spirits.

The entire episode was a life and death test to reveal his thoughts and feelings upon meeting such a disaster. The test determined whether or not he would retreat from his resolve for the Way. Would he entertain thoughts such as these: "Ha! I've been cultivating for so many years, reading Sutras, bowing repentances, burning a finger, living as a hermit, practicing all kinds of austerities, and my cultivation has been earnest, so why haven't I had the least response? Forget it! I'm giving up! I'm not going to cultivate any longer! I'm going to return to lay-life and indulge the five desires!" If he'd allowed such thoughts to occur, then he could

，過五欲的生活。」如果這樣一想，就不會做禪宗五宗的祖師了。

高旻寺的規矩最認眞，彼此不准講話，就是同住之人，也互相不知姓名。虛老在禪堂裏很守規矩，雖然病得很厲害，仍然隻字不提，也不說出落水被救的事，只是一心一意參禪。二十天後，病況好轉，此乃蒙佛菩薩之加被矣！

有一天，采石磯寶積寺住持德岸法師，來到高旻寺，發現虛老在凳上端然正坐，容光煥發，大爲驚悅，於是乎將虛老落水被救的事，向大眾宣布。眾人皆欽歎不已，爲成就虛老用功修行，於是禪堂內職，不令虛老輪值。至此，虛老更能一心參禪，直至一念不生的境地。

第八個七的第三天晚上，開靜時，當值斟開水，不愼將開水濺在虛老手上，於是手中茶杯落地，杯碎之聲，虛老聞而開悟（明朝時紫柏禪

never have become the Patriarch of the Five Sects of the Chan School.

The Venerable Hsu Yun obeyed the rules closely in the meditation hall, especially since Gaomin Monastery was noted for the extreme severity of its regulations. Nobody was allowed to hold conversations, and often it was the case that cultivators living side by side in the monastery would not even know each other's name. Venerable Hsu Yun was seriously ill, but did not mention the fact to anyone, nor did he tell the story about falling into the river. He only investigated Chan with a single-minded concentration. Twenty days passed, and his sickness abated, thanks to the aid bestowed upon him by the Buddhas and Bodhisattvas.

One day, the Venerable Master De An ("Virtue Shore"), the Abbot of Baoji Monastery at Cai Jetty, happened by the retreat at Gaomin, and he encountered the Venerable Hsu Yun, who was sitting upright and properly on the meditation bench, his face radiant and beaming. The Abbot De An was startled, and told the entire assembly about the incident of Venerable Master Hsu Yun's fall into the river and his rescue. After hearing the story the meditators expressed their unceasing admiration, and in order to allow Venerable Master Hsu Yun to cultivate successfully, they excused him from the rotation of administrative duties. Thus he was able to concentrate on his meditation single-mindedly, until he penetrated to a state of "no further thoughts arising."

On the third night of the eighth week, at the end of an hour of meditation, an attendant brought hot water around to serve to the sitters. As he poured a cup of water for the Venerable Master, he carelessly spilled some of the boiling water on the Master's hand. The teacup fell to the floor and shattered, and the Venerable Master

師聞碗碎聲而開悟），乃說偈曰：

　　　杯子撲落地，
　　　響聲明瀝瀝；
　　　虛空粉碎也，
　　　狂心當下歇。

　又說：

　　　燙著手，打碎杯，
　　　家破人亡語難開；
　　　春到花香處處秀，
　　　山河大地是如來。

開悟之後，虛老離開高旻寺，更努力精進，雲遊四方，勤訪善知識。後來到雲南，重修雞足山的寺院，因爲經費不足，所以到南洋去募款。搭船到新加坡時，在船上患病。下船後，因爲沒有護照，英國人認爲是傳染病，把他送到傳染病院；這也就是在該處等死的意思。後來才被送到極樂寺閉關，不久病漸得癒。後又到

Hsu Yun became enlightened upon hearing the sound of the cup shattering. (A similar event happened to Venerable Master Zibuo, "Purple Cedar," a Chan Master of the Ming Dynasty, who became enlightened at the sound of a shattering bowl). Venerable Master Hsu Yun spoke a verse on the spot:

> *Smashing with a clear, echoing sound,*
> *The teacup fell and hit the ground.*
> *Shattering empty space,*
> *The mad mind finally stops right there.*

And then he said another verse:

> *My hand was scalded, the cup shattered.*
> *The family's broken and relatives are gone—*
> *Words are hard to find.*
> *Spring's come now; buds are in bloom,*
> *Full and sweet in every place.*
> *Mountains, rivers, and the earth itself*
> *Are just the Thus Come One.*

After his enlightenment, he left Gaomin Monastery and cultivated even more vigorously than before, travelling extensively to look for and pay his respects to good and wise teachers. His travels carried him finally to Yunnan Province, where he rebuilt the monasteries on Jizu ("Chicken Foot") Mountain. Because his resources were insufficient, he journeyed on to Southeast Asia to solicit donations. The Venerable Master fell ill on the boat to Singapore, and, once ashore, the English inspectors interrogated him because he did not have a passport. They suspected that his illness was contagious and confined him in an isolation ward, where he was virtually left to die. However, later on he was sent to Jile ("Utmost Happiness") Monastery, where he went into seclusion, and, before long, regained

65

泰國募款，在某寺掛單，入定九天，似死而非
死，驚動泰京（曼谷），上自國王、大臣，下
至老百姓，都來皈依虛老。信徒供養，布施鉅
金，都匯回雲南，做爲建寺之需。

一九四七年春，南華寺傳戒，我才和虛老第一
次見面。現在還記得，傳完戒之後，虛老受了
點刺激，喉嚨發炎，不能説話，因此當時不便
詳問。經過醫生的治療，他才開始慢慢痊癒。

虛老一生，所受困苦艱難，眞是一言難盡！我
相信沒有任何人能夠經得起這種的折磨。他老
人家在這一世紀中，自度度他，自利利他，出
神入化、祥瑞之事，不勝枚舉。今天簡單向各
位介紹虛老一生的事蹟，希望各位學習他老人
家忍苦耐勞的精神。

現在的出家人，坐了幾天的禪，就想有感應，
就想開悟得大智慧，這未免貪心太大了。虛老
一生之中，捨死忘生，才把本來面目認識清楚

his health. Travelling on to Thailand to make his almsrounds, he stayed at a certain monastery and entered samadhi for nine days. His external appearance was lifeless, but in fact he was not dead. All Buddhists in Bangkok, the national capital, were startled by the news of his meditation skill; and the populace, from the King and his courtiers on down to the ordinary citizens, flocked to take refuge with the Venerable Hsu Yun. The offerings made by these faithful disciples were gathered into a lump sum and sent back to Yunnan, China, to finance the reconstruction of the monasteries.

In the spring of 1947, when Nanhua ("Southern China") Monastery held a precept ordination, I personally met the Venerable Master for the first time. I still remember the occasion: After the precepts had been transmitted, the Venerable Master Hsu Yun was stricken with a throat infection and lost his voice, so it was an inopportune time to hold a conversation. He was treated by the doctor and recovered slowly.

The troubles and miseries endured by the Venerable Master during his entire life were such that they could never be fully described in just a few sentences. I know beyond a doubt that few persons could have withstood the hardships and pressures that he endured. As he took both himself and others across, he benefitted both himself and others. The many miracles and spiritual marvels that he experienced throughout the century of his life span are too many to relate. I've given you only a brief sketch of his life, and I hope that in the future you will imitate the elder monk's untiring forbearance.

Left-home people of this day and age sit and meditate for a brief time and expect a response, or hope to get enlightened, and gain great wisdom. This is simply unrestrained greed. It took the Venerable Master Hsu Yun a lifetime of work to "see his original

虛雲老和尚
Great Master Hsu Yun

；我們受了什麼苦？做了什麼功德？就妄想開悟，簡直是幼稚的想法。

修道人，要志不退，願不退，行不退，一心一意向前精進，所謂「百尺竿頭，更進一步。」不管成就如何，只要發菩提心，努力修行，不要有所企圖，想得什麼五眼六通、神通妙用，這不是修行究竟的成果。切記！不要一天到晚，想神通，想開悟，那是修道的絆腳石。

一九八一年禪七 七月十六日至廿三日
開示於萬佛聖城萬佛殿

face," up to the point of forgetting all concern with life and death. What suffering have we undergone? What merit and virtue have we created? Yet we can still fantasize about getting enlightened! This is simply too childish!

Cultivators of the Way must never retreat from their resolve, from their vows, and from their practice. They must advance with single-minded vigor, so that "at the top of the hundred-foot pole, they take one more step." It does not matter what accomplishment you have. What counts is that you bring forth a great resolve for Bodhi, and work hard at your cultivation. Don't hanker after the Five Spiritual Eyes and Six Spiritual Penetrations, or the wonderful functioning of spiritual powers. They are not the ultimate reward of cultivation. Remember this well! Don't be thinking about gaining psychic powers and enlightenment from morning to night. Such thoughts are truly the stumbling block of cultivation!

A talk given during a Chan Session from July 16–23, 1981
The Hall of Ten Thousand Buddhas, The City of Ten Thousand Buddhas

宣化老禪師出家的因緣

從事譯經工作，乃是神聖的、
清高的、無上的。

【編按】：宣公上人是吉林省雙城縣人氏，俗姓
白，父富海公，一生勤儉治家，務農為業。母胡
太夫人，生前茹素念佛，數十年如一日，從未間
斷，為人好善樂施，為善最樂，有求必應，鄉里
稱讚不已，稱為活菩薩。戊午年三月十六日夜間
，太夫人夢見阿彌陀佛降臨，身放金光，照耀世
界，震動天地。驚醒之後，方覺異香撲鼻，香味
異常，清澈肺腑，真是不可思議的境界。不久，
宣公降生人間，連哭三天三夜而止，蓋覺娑婆世
界之苦不堪忍受故。今將宣公上人自述出家的因
緣，摘錄如下：

我在十二歲以前，脾氣很倔強，倔強到什麼程度
呢？凡是有人惹我的時候，就會哭，一哭起來，
就沒有完的時候。父母的話也不聽，非常任性，

The Story of the Venerable Master Hsuan Hua's Leaving the Home-life

Translating the Sutras is the work of the sages: it is exalted and supreme work.

Editor's Commentary: The Venerable Master Hsuan Hua is a native of Shuangcheng ("Twin Cities") County, Jilin ("Lucky Grove") Province, of Manchuria, China. He was surnamed Bai, His father, Mr. Bai Fuhai,was thrifty and frugal in managing the household, and was a farmer by occupation. His mother's maiden name was Hu. A vegetarian for her entire life, she recited the Buddha's name without cease for years, and was by nature a charitable and generous person who gave to anyone who asked. Her attitude was, "doing good deeds is the utmost happiness." As a result, her neighbors praised her constantly and gave her the name, "The Living Bodhisattva." On the night of the sixteenth day of the third lunar month, Mrs. Bai (Madame Hu) dreamed that Amitabha Buddha, his body shining with golden light that illuminated the entire world, came down, and the earth trembled and shook. Startled awake, she smelled an unusual fragrance that she had never known before. The scent was pure, and permeated her lungs and midriff; a truly inconceivable state of being. Soon after this experience, the Venerable Master was born. He cried incessantly for three days and three nights, perhaps feeling that the suffering of the Saha World was simply too painful for people to bear. The following is the Venerable Master's account of how he came to leave the home-life.

有時候不吃不喝，拼命地哭，令父母也沒有辦法
。當時的想法，知道父母非常疼愛我，我若是不
吃東西，父母的心會軟，會向我投降。我那時就
是這麼樣不孝，不能體會父母的辛苦，現在想起
來，實在不應該這麼樣不乖。

有一次，鄰居的小孩子來到我家，那時我剛會爬
，他也是在爬的階段，我們在炕上爬，看誰爬得
快？我爬到前頭，不料他用嘴來咬我的腳。愚笨
的我，不知反抗，只知道大哭，現在想起來，眞
可笑！

在十一歲那年，和同村的小朋友到郊外去玩，發
現一個嬰兒的屍體。我從來沒有見過這種事情，
認爲這小孩子在睡覺，但是叫也叫不醒，看他眼
睛閉著，又不喘氣，我莫名其妙，所以回家問母
親：「爲什麼小孩子在郊外睡覺呢？」母親說：
「那小孩子死了。」我又問：「爲什麼會死呢？
怎麼樣才不會死？」當時，有位親戚便說：「若
想不死，除非出家修道，才能不死。」那時候，

Before I reached age twelve, I was obstinate to the extreme. How stubborn was I? Whenever anyone provoked me, I'd always start to cry; and once I began to cry, I wouldn't stop. I disobeyed my parents, and did only what I pleased. Sometimes I refused to eat and drink, and cried my eyes out; my parents simply couldn't handle me. I knew at the time that my father and mother were very fond of me, and if I stopped eating, their hearts would yield, and I would get my way. That's how unfilial I was as a child. I had no appreciation of the trouble my parents went to on my behalf. Reflecting on my behavior, I regret that I was so naughty.

One day the neighbor's boy came over to play, and I'd just learned to crawl. He too, was a new toddler, and we both started to crawl on the bed; we held a race to see who could crawl faster. I took the lead, but then he started to bite my heels from behind. Stupid as I was, it didn't occur to me to resist or fight back; all I could do was to sob and cry. Thinking back on it, it was pretty funny!

In my eleventh year I went to the countryside with some other children to play, and discovered the dead body of a small child. Having never before witnessed the phenomenon of death, I assumed that the baby was just sleeping. When I called to it, however, it didn't wake up, and I noticed that its eyes were closed. Furthermore, its breath had stopped. I couldn't figure it out, and ran home to ask my mother what the matter was. "Why was the child sleeping out in the countryside?" I asked. She answered, "That child was dead." "Well, why do people die? How can they avoid dying?" I asked. A relative of the family who was visiting answered, "The only way to not die is to leave the home-life and cultivate the Way." The sight of death scared me, and I didn't want to die. The idea of undergoing round after round of birth and death seemed

我對死很怕，也就是不願意死，又覺得生生死死沒有意思，遂起了出家的念頭，想要去修道以了生脫死。

有一天，我對母親說：「我想出家修行，不知媽媽同不同意？」母親說：「出家是好事，我不能攔阻你。可是等我死後，你再出家也不遲。」母親已經許可我出家，我心中非常高興，但是不能即刻出家。當時的我，反省過去做了不知孝順父母的事，惹父母操心，令他們費了很多精神。怎樣來報答父母的養育之恩呢？我左想右想，想出一個笨法子——向父母叩頭，表示懺悔。想到這個，我就決定發這個心願。

當我開始給父母親叩頭的時候，我的父母嚇了一跳，便問：「爲什麼要叩頭？」我說：「因爲我以前不知孝順父母，惹父母生氣，現在知道不對了，所以從今天開始，向父母叩頭。」父親說：「既然知道錯，能改就好了，不必再叩頭了。」我說：「孩兒的個性一向倔強，說出的話，一定要做到。」父母親知道我的脾氣，不再說什麼，默許我的願心，接受我每天早晚叩頭。

meaningless, and I conceived the idea of leaving the home-life, since only by cultivating the Way can one put an end to birth and death.

One day I said to my mother, "I want to leave the home-life and cultivate the Way. Is that all right with you?" She said, "To leave home is a good thing, and I cannot prevent you from doing so. But I hope you will wait until after I die before you leave home; it won't be too late." Having obtained my mother's permission to leave home made me very happy, even though I could not fulfill my wish right away. At the time I reflected on my unfilial behavior in the past. I recalled how I had made my parents upset and wasted their energy in concern over me. I asked myself how I was going to repay their kindness in raising me and giving me my education. Tossing the question around in my mind, I struck upon a dumb idea: I would bow to them, to demonstrate my shame and remorse for my misbehavior. At that point, I decided to make a vow to do this.

As soon as I began to bow to them, my parents were startled, and asked me, "What are you bowing for?" I answered, "Because in the past, before I knew that I should be filial and respectful to my parents, I did many wrong things and made you both angry. Now I know I was wrong, and from today on, I am going to bow to you to make up for the past." My father said, "Since you already know that you were wrong, all you need to do is change; you don't have to keep on bowing like that." I responded, "I've always had a stubborn streak, and whatever I say, I will certainly do!" My parents were well-acquainted with my temperament; they didn't say anything, but silently complied with my wish and accepted the morning and evening bows that I made to them.

From then on, I'd rise early in the morning while the family was still

從此以後，每天清早起來（家人在睡覺時），就到院中向父親三叩頭，向母親三叩頭。每天晚間，家人上炕睡覺之後，就到院中向父母各叩三個頭。叩了一個時期，感覺不夠，於是又向天地叩頭。當時不知有天主、地主、人主等名詞，只知有天、地、君、親、師，所以每天早晚，給天叩三個頭，給地叩三個頭，給國家元首叩三個頭，給父親叩三個頭，給母親叩三個頭，給未來老師叩三個頭。這樣子叩頭，經過一段時期，感覺還不夠，又增加給天下大孝人叩頭，給天下大善人叩頭，給天下大賢人叩頭，給天下大聖人叩頭。以後又增加給全世界所有的好人叩頭，也給全世界所有的壞人叩頭。我對天叩頭，向天禱告，希望大惡、大壞的人，改惡遷善，統統成為好人。

這樣子增加下去，最後增加到八百三十個頭，每次要叩兩個半小時的頭，早晚兩次，需要五個小時。我在院中，無論颱風下雨，照叩不誤；就是冬天下雪，也是在院中叩頭，用我的愚誠來祈求風調雨順，國泰民安。

這樣叩了幾年，母親往生後，我在母親墓上守孝

in bed, and go out into the yard to bow three times to my father and three times to my mother. Each evening after my family had retired, I'd go out again and bow three times to each of my parents. Before long I felt that these bows were insufficient, and I added some bows to heaven and earth. At the time I had never heard the names of God, or earth-rulers, or kings among people; I knew only about heaven, earth, the emperor, parents, and teachers. So every morning and evening, I'd bow three times to heaven, three times to earth, three times to the leaders of the nation, three times to my father, three times to my mother, and three times to the teachers I would meet in the future. Time passed and I felt once more that this wasn't enough, so I increased my prostrations to include bows toward all the great filial sons and daughters on earth, and the great samaritans, and also the great worthies the world has known, and the great sages as well. The bows continued to expand to all the great good people, and even to all the great evil people in the world. While bowing to heaven, I made a wish that the really bad, evil people on earth would change their ways, reform, and become wholesome.

I kept adding bows in this way, until the total number of bows reached 830. The entire course of bows took two and a half hours to complete, and I bowed twice each day—morning and night. I spent five hours in the yard each day; regardless of rain or wind, the bowing still went on. Even during the winter while the snow fell, I continued to bow in the courtyard. I used a stupid sincerity to fuel my bowing, and I sought for the winds and rains to be regular and harmonious, for the country to be stable, and for the people to be at peace.

My practice of bowing continued for several years. After my

三年，仍然繼續叩頭。出家之後，開始研究經典，覺得佛經是世界上最完善的經典，也是世界上最豐富的經典，其他宗教的經典，簡直是望塵莫及。

我在未出家之前，參加各種宗教的活動，曾經參加天主教的彌撒儀式、基督教的安息會，還參加了旁門左道的法會。總而言之，到處尋覓了生脫死的方法，到最後很失望，找不到根本解決的方法，各宗教的教義，都不徹底、不究竟。但是發現天主教和基督教，能夠普遍令一般人所接受。為什麼？因為他們將《新約》和《舊約》，翻譯成各國文字，義理淺顯，容易明瞭。

佛教的教義，雖然很圓滿，但是文字太深，不是一般人所能明瞭，所以信仰的人很少。當時，我發了一個空願，決心將三藏十二部經典譯為白話文，再翻譯成世界各國文字。可是我不懂世界語言，也沒有機會學習，也沒有這種智慧，不知能否實現呢？

一九六二年，我來到美國弘揚佛法。到機緣成熟

mother passed away, I observed filial mourning by her graveside and continued bowing. The period of mourning completed, I left the home-life and began to study the Buddhist Sutras. These Sutras were, in my opinion, the most complete and wholesome texts on earth. I found them to be the richest and fullest resources. The spiritual classics of other religions were simply left in the dust; they couldn't compare.

Before I left the home-life, I occasionally joined the activities of other religions. I took part in a Catholic Mass and joined a Christian service. I also sat in the assemblies of the various heterodox sects and cults. To sum it up, I took every opportunity to look into the methods for resolving the matter of birth and death; and, frankly, I wound up disappointed by my inability to find any approach that dealt with the fundamental problem. The various methods proposed by the religions were not thoroughgoing and not ultimate. However, I realized that Catholicism and Christianity had been widely accepted by many people. Why? Because their *Old and New Testaments* had been translated into the languages of each country, and because the principles they contained were quite shallow and easy to understand.

The principles of Buddhism in the Sutras, although perfect and complete, were presented in very learned prose which was beyond the understanding of the average reader. Thus believers in Buddhism were very few. At this point, I made a futile vow, making up my mind to translate the entire Three Storehouses and Twelve Divisions of the Buddhist Canon into colloquial speech, and, further, to translate them into the languages of every nation on earth. The vow was "futile" because I myself didn't understand all the languages on earth, nor did I hope to get a chance to learn them.

時，美國弟子們，便開始翻譯經典，完成我的志願。經過多年的努力，翻譯的成績頗佳，可是離目標尚有一段距離，希望大家再接再厲，努力工作。從事這種使命，乃是神聖的、清高的、無上的。把三藏十二部全譯成英文，是功德無量的。

今天有位弟子發願，要將佛經翻譯成英文，讓我想起往日所發的願，盼望我的弟子，大家同心協力，來完成我所發的願力！

【編按】：宣公上人在南華寺親近虛老的時候，蒙老和尚重視，特委要職，受命為南華戒律學院監學，不久轉為教務主任。在傳戒時，為尊證阿闍梨。以後虛老將溈仰宗法脈傳上人，遂成為溈仰宗第九代接法人。

為續佛慧命，上人從香港來到美國，在美開演大乘經典數十部，提倡禪、教、律、密、淨五宗並重，打破門戶之見，以復興佛教為己任。並教導

I lacked this wisdom, and didn't know whether or not I could achieve my vow.

In 1962 I came to America to propagate the Buddhadharma, and when the opportunities ripened, my American disciples began the work of translation in order to fulfill my vow. After several years of effort, they've had a bit of success, but are still far short of the ultimate goal. I hope they will all forge ahead and work hard. If they can carry out this instruction, they will be doing the work of the sages; it is exalted and supreme work. The merit and virtue of this task, once the Three Stores of the Buddhist Canon are all translated into English, is truly limitless and boundless.

Today a disciple made a vow to translate the Buddhist Sutras into English, and it brought to mind the vow I made in the past. I hope that my disciples will work together and put their hearts and minds into the completion of my vow!

Note: At Nanhua Monastery, when the Venerable Master Hsuan Hua drew near to the Venerable Hsu Yun, he received the Elder's full attention, and was subsequently appointed as Director of the Nanhua Vinaya Academy. Soon the Master's duties were elevated to Director of Education. During the Precept Ordination Ceremonies, the Venerable Master Hua was asked to serve as Certifying Master (Acharya). Later on, the Elder Master Hsu Yun transmitted the "pulse of Dharma" of the Wei Yang Sect to the Venerable Master, making him the Ninth Patriarch of the Wei Yang Chan School.

In order to continue the Buddha's life of wisdom, the Venerable Master traveled from Hong Kong to America, where he has delivered lectures on several dozen Mahayana Sutras and promoted

弟子們天天要參禪打坐、念佛拜懺、研究經典，
眞實修行，以圖匡扶正教，令正法久住於世。

上人有超人的智慧，過目不忘的記憶力，講經說
法，事前不擬草稿，都是觀機逗教，因時、因地
、因事、因人而說。上人以無礙的辯才，口若懸
河，滔滔不絕，頭頭是道，說出來的義理圓融，
令人歎爲觀止。

上人講《華嚴經》時，能閉目念誦經文，一字不
錯，筆者認爲得未曾有，親目所見，親耳所聞，
所以衷心地敬佩。在上人座下的弟子，都是受過
高等教育的知識青年，對上人的德望學識，皆是
佩服得五體投地。

在上人德高望重之號召下，有華籍、美籍、越南
籍等各國青年男女，紛紛皈依受具、出家修道。
其中有博士學位、碩士學位，及學士學位者，他

the five main schools of Buddhism—Chan, Teachings, Vinaya, Secret, and Pure Land—with equal emphasis, eliminating the artificial separations between them. Taking the revitalization of Buddhism as his personal duty, he teaches his disciples that every day they must meditate, recite the Buddha's name, bow in repentance, investigate the Sutras, and genuinely cultivate in order to uphold the orthodox teaching and enable the proper Dharma to dwell long in the world.

The Venerable Master has peerless wisdom, and his memory retains at a glance any material that he reads. Before explaining the Sutras or speaking the Dharma, he has no need to prepare outlines or notes. Instead, he delivers his lectures according to the potentials that he perceives on the spot and talks to the audience based on the particular location, time, events, and people involved. His eloquence is truly unimpeded; the words pour forth in an unending stream, and every sentence tallies with the Way. The principles he elucidates are perfectly meshed and all-encompassing, and those who hear them praise them as worthy of deep consideration.

When the Venerable Master lectured on the *Flower Adornment Sutra*, he delivered the words of the text with his eyes closed, reciting from memory without being off by a single word. (I saw and heard the event with my own eyes and ears and felt it was unprecedented. It inspired my deep respect.) The assembly of disciples attending the Venerable Master's lectures include many intelligent, well-educated young people, who display the utmost respect and admiration for the Venerable Master's virtuous conduct and his erudition.

The young men and women who have responded to the Venerable Master's reputation for excellent virtue and strict standards include

們放下前程似錦的生活，入佛門求證眞理。有的修苦行打餓七，或二十一日禁食，或三十六日禁食，或七十二日禁食。這種苦行在美國佛教史上是空前的壯舉，希有之至！又有的爲祈禱世界和平，發願三步一拜，二年六個月，從未間斷，風雨不誤，身體力行，做一切佛教徒之榜樣。這些都是因爲受上人高蹈懿行所感動，而發心效法上人這種行菩薩道，爲人忘我的精神。

上人教導有方，弟子們循規蹈矩，認眞修行，遵守佛制，時時搭衣、日中一食、夜不倒單。可以說，全世界現在找不到第二個地方；所以萬佛聖城是世界的佛教中心，對所有佛弟子有不可思議的啓迪作用。

上人於一九六二年，攜正法西來，歷年來創辦法界佛教總會（前身爲中美佛教總會），又成立萬佛聖城及美、加、臺、馬等地各分支道場。爲培養世界棟樑之材，特在萬佛聖城設立法界佛教大學、培德中學、育良小學。爲令正法久住，造就行解兼顧之佛教人材，遂設立僧伽居士訓練班。爲使佛經流通於全世界，又成立國際譯經學院，

natives of China, America, Vietnam, and other countries, who have come to take the Three Refuges and the Complete Precepts, to leave the home-life, and to cultivate the Way. They include holders of Bachelor's, Master's and Doctoral degrees, and many have renounced lucrative occupations and luxurious lifestyles in the world to study the true principles of the Buddhadharma. Some cultivate asceticism, with fasting of one week, or three weeks; some fast as long as thirty-six days, and even up to seventy-two days. Such a vigorous ascetic regimen is unparalleled in the history of Buddhism in America, and can be considered extremely rare! There are also some who, for the sake of world peace, have vowed to bow once every three steps, and they have done so continuously for two and a half years. Undaunted by the wind or rain, they practice this in order to serve as models for all Buddhists. Inspired by the Venerable Master's exalted virtuous conduct, they strive to emulate the Master's spirit of forgetting himself for the sake of others to practice the Bodhisattva Way.

The Venerable Master's teaching methods are effective; his disciples are well-behaved. They cultivate earnestly and observe the Buddha's regulations of always wearing their precept-robes, eating one meal a day at noon, and not lying down to sleep. It would be hard to find another place with comparable standards. Therefore, the City of Ten Thousand Buddhas has become a center of world Buddhism and serves as an inspiration for all Buddhists.

In 1962, the Venerable Master brought the Proper Dharma to the West, and in the years that followed, he founded the Dharma Realm Buddhist Association (formerly the Sino-American Buddhist Association), the City of Ten Thousand Buddhas, and other Way-places in the United States, Canada, Taiwan, Malaysia, and other

現有許多僧尼、居士，埋頭苦幹，致力於將佛經翻譯爲英文。現已出版一百餘部中、英及其他西方語文之經書，流通世界各地。

上人一生堅苦卓絶，爲法忘軀。時至今日，法界佛教總會之分支道場，雖已遍及美、加與亞洲各地，然而上人仍保持一貫謙遜淡泊之態度，自稱是「一隻小螞蟻」，處在人人之下，絶對不和任何人爭。他曾説：「萬佛聖城不是私人的機構，是屬於全世界佛教徒所有，甚至全世界宗教徒也包括在内。目前在聖城的住衆，終日埋頭苦幹，我只是做一個守門人，一個清道夫，等著有緣的衆生到這裏共同修行。你們不要把自己抛到門外，你們都是萬佛聖城的成員，將來都要成佛。」

一九八一年禪七 七月十六日至廿三日
開示於萬佛聖城萬佛殿

countries. In order to educate people to become good citizens of the world, at the City of Ten Thousand Buddhas the Venerable Master established Dharma Realm Buddhist University, Developing Virtue High School, and Instilling Goodness Elementary School. For the sake of causing the Proper Dharma to remain in the world and to train Buddhist workers in both theory and practice, he established the Sangha and Laity Training Programs. He also founded the International Translation Institute so that Buddhist Sutras might circulate throughout the world. Many monks, nuns, and laypeople are now diligently working to translate the Sutras into English. Over a hundred volumes of Sutras and Buddhist texts have already been published in Chinese, English, and other languages and are being circulated worldwide.

The Master's whole life has been one of hardship and distinctive achievement, of selfless dedication to the Dharma. Although the branch monasteries of Dharma Realm Buddhist Association have spread throughout the United States, Canada, and Asia, the Venerable Master remains as humble and modest as ever, calling himself a tiny ant that walks beneath everyone else and would never contend with anyone. He has said, "The City of Ten Thousand Buddhas is not a private institution; it belongs to all the Buddhists of the world, and in fact, the followers of all religions have a share in it. The people living at the City of Ten Thousand Buddhas are putting their nose to the grindstone everyday; I am just the person who watches the door, a custodian waiting for those living beings who have affinities to come here and cultivate together. None of you should stand outside the door and be afraid to come in; all of you are members of the City of Ten Thousand Buddhas, and in the future you will become Buddhas.

A talk given during a Chan Session from July 16-23, 1981
The Hall of Ten Thousand Buddhas, The City of Ten Thousand Buddhas

果佐行者出家的因緣

安分守己，老老實實，勤加修持，
才能得到真功夫。

我在哈爾濱南三十里平房站三緣寺時，有一天在
定中觀察，知道第二天有個小孩子會來出家。第
二天早上，我就對弟子果能說：「今天會有個小
孩子來出家。等他來了，告訴我！」中午時，果
能到我房中，用山東腔說：「師父！您說的那個
小孩子，真地來了！」我到前邊一看，是個十二
、三歲的男孩子，五官端正，身體強壯，看起來
是比丘相。這個男孩見到我，好像見到久別的親
人一般，情不自禁地就哭起來了，所謂「喜極而
泣」。

我問他：「你為什麼要出家？」小孩子說：「因
為我有病（他在五歲時，能替人家治病，可是自
己有病，不能治自己的病），醫生檢查不出病源
，束手無策，無藥可治。父母非常著急，到處求
醫仍不見效。有一天夜裏，我連作三個相同的夢

The Story of Cultivator Guo Zuo's Leaving the Home-life

Being content with our station, guarding our behavior, and truly cultivating with vigorous energy is only way to attain actual skill.

While staying at Sanyuan ("Three Conditions") Monastery, which was located south of Harbin, thirty (Chinese) miles away, at the town of Pingfang Station, I saw in my meditative contemplation that the following morning a young boy would come to leave the home-life. The next morning I told my disciple Guo Neng, "Today, a young boy is coming to leave home. Tell me when he arrives." At noon, Guo Neng came to my room and said in his Shandong accent, "Teacher, that boy you mentioned has finally come!" I went down to the front hall and found a strapping boy of twelve or thirteen whose build and countenance were handsome and full; he had the look of a Bhikshu. The boy took one look at me and couldn't control his emotions. Just like one who sees a long-lost relative, he began crying uncontrollably, shedding tears of joy.

"Why do you want to leave home?" I asked him. "Because I have a serious illness," he answered. From the age of five, he could cure others' illnesses, but he couldn't cure his own illness. "Doctors couldn't find the reason for my ailment and had no medicine to heal me. They were at a loss as to what to do. My father was very anxious. He sought a cure everywhere, but nothing seemed to work. One night I had the same dream three times, in which I saw a fat monk who came to me and said, 'Your illness will never be cured

89

，在夢中有位胖和尚，對我說：『你的病，除非到哈爾濱三緣寺去找安慈法師，跟他出家修道，即能不藥而癒。否則的話，是沒有希望的。』我清清楚楚地記得，所以徵求父母的同意了，來到這裏。請安慈法師慈悲，收我為弟子。」

當時，我笑著對他說：「你認識安慈法師嗎？」

他說：「我不認識。」

我說：「既然你不認識，你怎能找到他呢？我們這裏沒有安慈法師。」

小孩子很有信心地說：「不會吧！剛才我進門時，就看見夢中那位胖和尚坐在那裏（他用手指著彌勒菩薩），他不會騙人的。是他教我來的，絕對不會錯。」

我又問他：「你所說的夢話，有什麼根據令人相信？你是不是沒有衣服穿，沒有飯吃，沒有地方住，想來出家？」

他堅定地說：「不是的！我是受胖胖和尚的指示，教我來找安慈法師，只有他才能醫好我的病。所以，我走了一個多月，步行一千多里。（當時

unless you go to the Sanyuan Monastery in Harbin and leave the home-life to cultivate the Way under Dharma Master An Tse. If you do that, you will be cured spontaneously, without medicine. If you don't do this, you have no hope of recovery.' The memory of the dream was quite clear, so I obtained my father's permission to come here and seek the compassion of Dharma Master An Tse, to allow me to leave home."

I laughed, and asked him, "Do you know Dharma Master An Tse?"

"No, I don't," he said.

I said, "I'm afraid there is no Dharma Master An Tse here."

"Oh yes, there is!" The lad answered confidently. "As soon as I entered the door I saw that same fat monk who was in my dream. He's sitting right over there." (The boy pointed to Maitreya Bodhisattva.) "He wouldn't cheat anybody. He told me to come here; there's no mistake."

"What proof do you have that this dream-talk is true? Who will believe you?" I challenged him. "You're probably just a poor boy with no clothes, food and shelter, who wants to come and leave the home-life, aren't you?"

"No, I'm not!" he replied firmly. "I'm simply following the instructions of that fat monk, and he directed me to look for Dharma Master An Tse; he's the only one who can cure my disease. That's why I've been on the road for over a month, walking one thousand miles to get here." (At that time the Japanese had just surrendered unconditionally, and the railroads in Manchuria had not yet resumed operation.)

"Sometimes along the road I walked right past the last inn in a

日本無條件投降，東北的鐵路已經不通車。）有時候，走過旅店，前邊沒有村莊，只好在荒地上睡覺。爲趕時間，不顧一切，有一天夜裏，我在草坪上睡覺，忽然有狼群，很快將我包圍在中間，可是我不怕，我對狼群說：「快點離開！不然，我對你們不客氣，給你們個彈（手榴彈）吃。」這時，狼群就乖乖地走了，這是他求法的一個小插曲。

他說完經過之後，用乞求的眼光看著我。我要考驗他是否有誠意，於是將饅頭用口嚼爛，吐在地上，對他說：「你把它撿起來，吃下去，吃完再說。」他毫不考慮，也不嫌口水骯髒，撿起來就吞到肚中。他這個考試及格了，證明他是誠心誠意來出家，於是我給他授了沙彌戒，成爲一個小沙彌。

他受戒（沙彌戒）之後，用功修行，勇猛學習，毫不懈怠，又不放逸，不到半年的時間，便證得五眼六通，本事很高，可以說是神通廣大。這不是誇大之詞，是千眞萬確的事實，當時的人，皆知這個小沙彌有神通。可惜他後來生出貢高我慢

town, and found no village ahead, so I could only camp out in the open fields. I was in a hurry to get here, and I paid no attention to anything else. One night I was sleeping in a meadow when suddenly a pack of wolves surrounded me. I wasn't afraid of them, though, and I said, 'Get out of here, or else I'm going to give you trouble. You're going to get a taste of these eggs (hand grenades)!' And the pack of wolves ran away obediently."

Having said his piece, he looked up at me with pleading eyes. I decided to give his sincerity another test. I picked up a piece of steamed bread and, after chewing it up thoroughly, spit it out on the ground. I said, "First pick that up and eat it, then we'll see what's what." He didn't hesitate for an instant or worry about my unsanitary saliva, but promptly scooped up the bread and swallowed it down. Having passed his test, he had demonstrated that his wish to leave the home-life was sincere. I gave him the Novice Precepts, and he became a young Shramanera.

Having received the Precepts, he worked hard in his cultivation. He was quite a courageous student, not at all lax or lazy. Before six months passed, he realized the attainment of the Five Eyes and Six Spiritual Penetrations. His skill was considerable, and his psychic abilities were vast. This is not an exaggeration, but a matter of absolute fact. Everyone in the area knew that this young novice monk had psychic powers. It is sad that afterwards he fell into arrogance and pride. He grew haughty, and his psychic abilities vanished. When he wanted to demonstrate them, he couldn't do so anymore.

Cultivators of the Way must pay close attention to this. Whether we have psychic powers or not, we shouldn't indulge in pride or

的心、自滿的心，認爲自己了不起，所以神通就不翼而飛，要顯也顯不出來了。

我們修道人要注意，無論有神通也好，沒有神通也好，千萬不要生驕傲的心、執著的心，更不可以自我宣傳，自賣廣告。要安分守己，老老實實去精進，勤加修持，才能得到真功夫。千萬不可在皮毛上用功夫，聽到什麼音聲，看到什麼境界，便認爲了不起，要曉得那離真道還有十萬八千里呢！

一九八一年禪七 七月十六日至廿三日
開示於萬佛聖城萬佛殿

attachments for any reason whatsoever! Even less should we advertise for ourselves and create our own publicity. Our proper role is to be content with our station, guard our behavior, and truly, honestly, cultivate with vigorous energy. Be valiant and forge ahead; that's the only way to attain actual spiritual skill. Under no circumstances may we toy with the superficial aspects, and when provoked by a certain sound, or struck by a certain vision, feel that we have become extraordinary. To make such a mistake leaves the true Way a million miles away!

A talk given given during a Chan Session from July 16-23, 1981
The Hall of Ten Thousand Buddhas, The City of Ten Thousand Buddhas

果舜行者出家的因緣

念念莫忘生死苦，心心想脫輪迴圈。

果舜是吉林省哈爾濱市人，俗姓姚，以農爲業。夙秉善根，感覺世界，萬苦交煎，充滿罪惡，乃萌出世之念，到處訪求明師。有一天，在途中被日本兵（僞滿時代）發現，認爲是無業遊民，強迫送到邊界去做苦工。

他被送到黑河勞工營中，時時想逃走，可是找不到機會。因爲營房的四周，用電網圍繞，如有逃者，不是被守兵槍擊而死，就是被狼犬所咬死，縱使僥倖逃過此二關，也逃不出電網，一定被電所燒死。這等於人間地獄一樣，苦不堪言。

有一天晚上，果舜在夢中，見到有位長鬚老人對他說：「今天晚上是你出離樊籠的時機，在門外有隻白狗，隨牠而去！」果舜驚醒，悄悄走到門外，果然見到有隻白狗，在等著他。於是乎他就

96

The Story of Cultivator Guo Shun's Leaving the Home-life

In every moment, do not forget the suffering of birth and death. In every thought, yearn to escape the wheel of transmigration.

Guo Shun was a native of Jilin (Lucky Grove) Province in China and made his home in the city of Harbin. His surname was Yao, and he was a farmer by occupation. His good roots from lives past led him to realize that the world was full of trials and suffering. His sensitivity to the evils that filled the world gave him the wish to leave the home-life. To realize this wish, he travelled about to seek wise teachers. One day (during the Japanese occupation of Manchuria) a patrol of Japanese soldiers found him, mistook him for a vagrant, and ordered to work in the countryside.

He was sent to the Li River forced-labor camp. Imprisoned there, his only wish was to escape, but he never got a chance. An electrified fence encircled the camp, and any person who attempted to escape was either shot to death by the guards, or was savagely attacked by killer dogs that patrolled the perimeters. Even if by sheer luck one escaped the sentries and the watchdogs, there was still the electric fence that immolated anyone who touched it. The camp was a small hell on earth, dreadful to the extreme.

One night while sleeping, Guo Shun dreamed of a long-bearded old man who told him, "Tonight is your chance to escape this cage. There's a white dog outside the door. Follow him and run away!" Startled awake, Guo Shun tiptoed to the doorway, and sure enough,

跟隨狗的後邊，安全走出電網，逃回家鄉。他慶幸死裏逃生，又看破紅塵，所以決心出家修道。

民國三十三年冬天，我到大南溝屯爲高居士的母親治病。第二天，全屯傳遍高母病癒之奇蹟。這個時候，果舜聽聞了，就想來拜我爲師。他長跪不起，我見他很誠心，所以允許他的請求，滿他的心願，並對他開示：「在家修道不易，出家修道更難，所謂『大事未明，如喪考妣；大事已明，更如喪考妣。』修行人還要忍人所不能忍，受人所不能受，吃人所不能吃，穿人所不能穿。要勤修戒定慧，息滅貪瞋癡，這是沙門的本分。」又爲他說一首偈頌：

念念莫忘生死苦，
心心想脫輪迴圈；
虛空粉碎明佛性，
通體脫落見本源。

又對他開示：「現在是末法時代，出家者多，修道者少；信佛者多，成佛者少。你既然發願出家，必要發菩提心，做疾風中之硬燭，烈火內之精

saw a white dog waiting for him just outside. He walked behind the dog safely past the electrified fence, and made it all the way home without difficulty. Snatched from the jaws of death, he saw through the illusion of the material world and deeply resolved to leave the home-life to cultivate the Way.

In the winter of 1944, I went to the village of Danangou (Big Southern Ditch) to cure Upasaka Gao's mother's illness. The following day, news of the woman's miraculous recovery spread throughout the village. When the story reached Guo Shun, he came to ask me to be his teacher. He knelt down and did not rise. Seeing his sincerity, I permitted him to leave home, thus fulfilling his wish. I gave him these instructions: "It is not easy to cultivate at home, and to cultivate as a left-home person is harder still. It's said that,

> *Before the great matter is clear to you,*
> *you feel as if you have lost your parents.*
> *After you understand the great matter,*
> *you feel even more as if you have lost your parents.*

Cultivators must endure what other people cannot endure; they must take on what others cannot take on; they must eat what others are unable to eat, and wear what others are unable to wear. The Shramana's duty is to diligently cultivate precepts, concentration, and wisdom, and to put an end to greed, hatred, and stupidity.

> *In every moment, do not forget the suffering of birth and death.*
> *In every thought, yearn to escape the wheel of transmigration.*
> *Obliterate empty space and understand the Buddha-nature.*
> *Cast off the entire substance and see the original source.*

I gave him further instructions: "We are now in the age of the Dharma's decline. Although there are still many people who leave home, those who actually cultivate the Way are very few. People

99

金，不可辜負出家之初衷，謹之！慎之！」於是果舜叩頭頂禮，跟我到三緣寺受沙彌戒，法名為果舜。果舜出家之後，勇猛精進，嚴守戒律，不懈怠、不放逸，但專一其心，參禪打坐。每次入定，往往經過一晝夜的時間而出定，在定中能知過去、現在、未來一切的因果，這是很不可思議的境界。

民國三十四年九月，果舜在大南溝屯的西山下，龍王廟之左，自建茅棚，做為自修之所。落成之日，我率領果能、果佐、果植等去開光，當天夜裏，有十位龍神來請求皈依。我對他們說：「汝等職列水祇，受人供養。天時如此奇旱，因何不雨？」諸龍神異口同聲地說：「無玉帝敕命，小神不敢擅行降雨。」我就對他們說：「汝等代吾奏帝釋（玉皇大帝），請求明日降雨，然後再為汝等授皈依。」第二天，果然天降大雨，解除旱災，農民歡喜若狂，感謝神恩，唱戲為酬，人神同樂。

因為果舜茅棚開光，有此一段因緣，所以命名為「龍雨茅蓬」，以誌紀念。

who believe in the Buddha are many, but very few actually become Buddhas. Since you have now made a decision to leave home, you must make the resolve for Bodhi. Be like a bright candle in a strong gale; be like refined gold in a smelting furnace. Do not fail your initial inspiration to leave home. Work hard, and take care."

Guo Shun bowed to me and then followed me to Sanyuan (Three Conditions) Monastery to receive the Shramanera (novice) precepts; I gave him the Dharma-name of Guo Shun. After he became a monk, he made courageous, vigorous progress. He held the precepts strictly, and was never remiss or lazy. He concentrated his mind in meditation practice. Every time he entered samadhi, he would sit for an entire day and night. While in that state of concentration, he could know the causes and results of all things in the past, the present, and the future. His state was inconceivable.

In September of 1945, Guo Shun built a cottage to the left of Dragon King Temple, below West Mountain, near Danangou Village, in order to cultivate in seclusion. I took disciples Guo Neng, Guo Zuo, Guo Zhi, and others to inaugurate the temple on the opening day. On that very night, ten dragon spirits came to me seeking to become "refuge disciples." I told them, "You all have the duty of bringing rain and receiving people's offerings. There is an unseasonal drought here now. Why hasn't it rained for so long?" The dragon spirits answered in unison, "Unless the Jade Emperor gives us the order, we little spirits don't dare to randomly make the rain fall." I said to them, "Please relay my request for rain tomorrow to the Jade Emperor. Then I'll let you take refuge." The next day, as it turned out, there was a rainstorm, and the drought came to an end, which set the local farmers dancing for joy. They celebrated with songs and festivities to thank the spirits for their kindness, and everyone was quite happy about the whole thing.

茅棚中共有三人同修，是同村人。劉居士和楊居士，隨果舜作早晚功課，以誦〈大悲咒〉爲主課。後來劉居士出家爲僧；楊居士被徵，參加八路軍，參軍之後，常常寫信回家，以後消息突然斷絕，家人十分惦念，懷疑彼已不在人間。

民國三十七年某日，果舜和高居士在茅棚中誦〈大悲咒〉，忽然聽見有人叫門的聲音，開門一看，原來是楊居士回來了。他一言不發，就到屋後去了。果舜繼續誦〈大悲咒〉，誦畢，到屋後去看楊居士，想問他這兩年到哪兒去了？一進門，就看見一隻狐狸，挾尾而逃。

果舜因爲持〈大悲咒〉，已具威德，狐狸無法擾亂其心，乃現原形。大概是因爲楊居士在戰場死了，其頭腦被狐狸所噬，所以現楊居士之形來引誘。豈知果舜的定力到了不動轉的程度，邪不侵正，狐狸精始知難而退。所以修道人要經得起考驗，不要被境界所轉。

民國三十四年七月十五日盂蘭盆法會，我率領弟子，在佛前燃香，我乃發願：「若能活到百歲，

These were the circumstances that commemorated the events surrounding the dedication of Guo Shun's cottage, which was thereupon named Dragon Rain Cottage.

Three people lived and cultivated there, all of whom were neighbors from the same town. Two laymen, Mr. Liu and Mr. Yang, did morning and evening ceremonies with Guo Shun, and they recited the Great Compassion Mantra as their primary method of cultivation. Layman Liu later left home to join the Sangha, and layman Yang was drafted into the Eighth Route Army. After becoming a soldier, he regularly sent letters home, but one day the letters suddenly stopped, much to the anxiety of the entire family; they assumed right away that their boy was no longer alive.

One afternoon in 1948, Guo Shun and Mr. Gao were reciting the Great Compassion Mantra in the hut when they heard a knock on the door. They opened it to find that Mr. Yang had returned. He walked in without saying a word, and continued on to the back of the building. Guo Shun continued to recite the Great Compassion Mantra until the end of the hour. Then he went to the room at the back to see Mr. Yang, and asked where he had been during the last two years. When they entered the room they saw a fox that shook its tail and ran out.

Because Guo Shun recited the Great Compassion Mantra and led a life of virtue, the fox had no way to disturb his mind, and could only revert to its true identity. They surmised that Mr. Yang had been killed on the battlefield, and his brain had been eaten by a fox. That animal later came to their cottage to make mischief disguised as Mr. Yang. The fox spirit didn't expect that Guo Shun's samadhi-strength was already imperturbable, and that he could not be overpowered by the deviant magic. The fox spirit met its match and

103

則燒全身，供養佛陀，求無上道。」當時每個弟子，都發心願。果舜也發願：「弟子果舜！若遇相當機會，願效藥王菩薩，燃身供佛，不待百歲。」我在觀察中知道他宿有此願，所以允許他發這個願。

民國三十八年四月十八日，果舜感覺一切無常，而佛教破產，痛不堪言，悲不忍睹，乃發心燃身，以殉教難。自備油柴，端坐其上，自焚其身。次日，村人方知，大家來看，果舜已全身成灰，唯心未焚化。村人敬之，於是將其骨灰及心埋葬於殉難之處。

一九八一年禪七　七月十六日至廿三日
開示於萬佛聖城萬佛殿

ran away in defeat. The story illustrates that cultivators must face all kinds of tests and take care not to be moved by circumstances.

On the fifteenth of the seventh lunar month in 1945, the day of the Ullambana celebration, I led a group of disciples to offer incense to the Buddhas and make this vow: "If I am allowed to live to the age of one hundred, I will burn my entire body as an offering to the Buddha, in quest of the supreme Way." All of the disciples present at the time made the same vow. Guo Shun also made the vow, "Disciple Guo Shun vows that if the opportunity appears, I will imitate Bodhisattva Medicine King and burn my entire body as an offering to the Buddha; I will not wait until my hundredth year before making this offering." Through my meditative contemplation, I knew that he made this vow in past lives as well, so I permitted him to make the same vow this time.

On April 18, 1949, Guo Shun felt that all in the world was impermanent and that Buddhism had grown decadent. His pain at seeing these two truths was bitter beyond words. His grief was indescribable. Thus he vowed to burn his body, to die for the sake of Buddhism. He gathered a pile of tinder, soaked it with oil, sat on top of it in the meditation posture, then burned himself. The next day, when news of the event reached the local people, everyone came out for a look. Guo Shun's entire body had burned to ashes; only his heart remained unburnt. The villagers respected him greatly, and they buried his ashes and heart in the place where he had given up his life.

A talk given during a Chan Session from July 16-23, 1981
The Hall of Ten Thousand Buddhas, The City of Ten Thousand Buddhas

修道的六大宗旨

正法就是不爭、不貪、不求、不自私、不自利、不打妄語。

修道人要有擇法眼，才能選擇何爲正法，何爲邪法。正法就是不爭、不貪、不求、不自私、不自利、不打妄語，這是修道人的六大宗旨。依此宗旨去修行，就是正知正見。邪法就是有爭、有貪、有求、有自私、有自利、打妄語。有了這六種心，就是邪知邪見。正邪的關鍵在於此，所以這是正邪的分水嶺；向前流是正法，向後流是邪法。這一點，大家要認清楚。

如果沒有邪知邪見，只要你的定力堅固，不論魔王如何來擾亂，不會動搖你的道心，所謂「佛來佛斬，魔來魔斬。」爲什麼要這樣說？因爲教你不要執著境界，就是佛來，也不接受，何況是魔呢？在境界中的預兆，雖然有時很靈驗，可是不要相信。那麼要相信什麼？就相信不爭、不貪、

The Six Great Guidelines for Cultivating the Way

The proper dharmas are: not fighting, not being greedy, not seeking, not being selfish, not wanting personal advantages, and not telling lies.

Cultivators of the Way must possess "Dharma-selecting vision" in order to distinguish proper dharmas from deviant dharmas. The proper dharmas are: not fighting, not being greedy, not seeking, not being selfish, not wanting personal advantages, and not telling lies. These are known as the Six Great Guidelines. When one bases his cultivation on these Six Guidelines, he is equipped with proper knowledge and views. Deviant dharmas are simply fighting, greed, seeking, selfishness, wanting personal advantages, and telling lies. One who has these six thoughts possesses deviant knowledge and views. Proper and deviant swings on the hinge-pin of these points. They are the standard for distinguishing the proper from the deviant. Water that flows forward represents the proper Dharma; water that flows backwards represents deviant Dharma. All of you should recognize this point very clearly.

If you are free of deviant knowledge and views and your samadhi is solid, then no matter how the demon kings come to bother you, your resolve for cultivation will not waver. A saying goes, "If the Buddhas come, slay the Buddhas. If the demons come, slay the demons." What does this mean? It means you should not become attached to states. If the Buddha appears, don't go out to receive him; how much less should you welcome a demon. Although such

107

不求、不自私、不自利、不妄語。這六種宗旨，就是六把斬魔劍、降魔杵。

有了這種正知正見之後，就算有天人現身來供養、來叩頭，也不動心。如果一動心，或生出歡喜心，歡喜魔便得其方便，令你發狂。若生憂愁心，那麼憂愁魔就得其方便，乘機而入，來擾亂你的心，令你煩惱。或者生了執著心，或者生了我慢心，都會受魔來擾亂，使思想不清淨。

所以無論遇到什麼奇奇怪怪的境界，不要相信，不要動心。要相信自己的智慧，要明白自性能生萬法，自性本來清淨，自性本無染污，自性本不顛倒。若能這樣，還有什麼可求呢？凡是有所求，就是染污；有爭、有貪、有自私、有自利、打妄語，都是染污。無論什麼法，都可以用這六大宗旨做為尺度，來衡量、來觀察，合者是正法，不合者是邪法。

這六大宗旨，能破天魔外道的邪知邪見。天魔外道所行所作，皆有所求。總是在爭、貪、求、自

states are occasionally premonitions, all the same, do not believe in what you experience. What should we believe in, then? Believe in not fighting, not being greedy, not seeking, not being selfish, not being self-indulgent, and not telling lies.

These Six Guidelines are six demon-slaying swords, six demon-quelling pestles. After you possess such proper knowledge and views, then even if gods from the heavens were to appear to you, make offerings, and bow in respect, you would not let your thoughts waver. If your thoughts did waver and you felt happy about it, then a demon of happiness could gain control of you, seize the opportunity to upset your cultivation, and drive you insane. If you were to get worried, then a demon of worry could use this opportunity to gain control of you, disturb your mind, and cause you to get afflicted. If you were to become attached or arrogant, you would also come under the disturbing influence of demons. The result in each case is that your thoughts would be rendered impure.

Therefore, no matter what strange and uncanny situations occur to you, don't believe that any of them are real, and don't allow them to disturb your thoughts. Believe only in your own wisdom. Know that your own nature is capable of bringing into being all the myriad things of creation. Know that this inherent nature is basically pure and free of defilement; know that it is fundamentally free of inversion. If you can see things this way, then what is there to seek? Anything you sought would be a defilement. Anything that comes about from fighting, greed, seeking, selfishness, self-indulgence or dishonesty is certainly corrupt. No matter what dharma it is, you may use the Six Guidelines to as a yardstick to measure, judge, and contemplate it. If it accords with the six rules, it can be called a proper dharma. If it goes against them, it is a deviant dharma.

私、自利、妄語中打主意，一切爲自己，而不爲
他人，這就是旁門左道的思想。

修道人要行所無事，積功累行，不可執著，所謂
「掃一切法，離一切相。」不可以說：「我有什
麼功夫，我有什麼修行。」或者說：「我有什麼
境界，我有什麼神通。」就算是有的話，都是虛
妄不實，不可相信的，不要上當了。若相信異端
神通，就不能成就正定正受。要曉得正定正受不
是從外邊得來，乃是從自性中生出來的。怎樣能
生出來？就是迴光返照，反求諸己，才能有所成
就。

萬佛聖城是萬聖聚會的地方，可是在四周也有魔
王在等待機會。如果有修道人心不清淨，盡打妄
想，魔王就入其竅，做你的顧問，譬如令你預先
知道今天尚未發生的事。你若認爲這是神通，就
上了魔王的大當，成爲他的眷屬。

不要聽到一點聲音，便認爲虛空在說話。虛空本
來無言語，所謂「離言說相，離心緣相。」假如

The Six Guidelines can destroy the deviant knowledge and views of the celestial demons and externalists. The deeds of celestial demons and externalists are all characterized by seeking. Their actions always center around contention, greed, seeking, selfishness, self-indulgence and dishonest behavior. They do things only for themselves, never for others. Thinking like this is typical of deviant cults.

People who cultivate the Way should act as if nothing is being done. We want to amass merit and virtue, but not be attached to the process. It is said: "Sweep away all dharmas; go beyond all attachment to views." It's wrong to say, "I have this particular spiritual skill," or "I have some cultivation." It's wrong to say, "I have such and such a state," or "I have such and such a psychic power." Even if you have such attainment, it is still unreal and not to be believed. Do not be taken in. Faith in strange, miraculous abilities and psychic powers will keep you from realizing genuine "proper concentration and proper reception" (samadhi). You should realize that proper concentration and proper reception does not come from outside, but is born instead from within your own nature. How does one bring it into being? Only by instropection and reflection, by seeking within oneself, can it be achieved.

The City of Ten Thousand Buddhas is a place where ten thousand sages gather. On all sides, however, demon-kings also gather, waiting for their chance. If the thoughts of a cultivator should be impure, should he or she indulge in idle thinking, the demon king will slip right in and act as the cultivator's advisor. He may, for example, inform you of events that have not yet taken place, giving you foreknowledge. If you should assume that this knowledge amounts to psychic powers, then you will have been seriously

111

聽到虛空有聲音，那就是魔的境界，不是大圓鏡智所應該有的。爲什麼要耽著雕蟲小技？這是沒有出息的行爲。

修道人心要清淨，不要貪圖預先知道的事。先知道將要發生什麼，反而有麻煩，這令你分心，精神不能集中，無法專一來修道，妄想紛飛，煩惱重重。不知道，不煩惱，就無罣礙。在《心經》上說：「無罣礙故。無有恐怖。遠離顛倒夢想。究竟涅槃。」這才是修道人所應趣向的目標。

tricked, duped by the demon king, and you will become one of his followers.

Don't let it be the case that you hear some sounds and assume that voices are talking with you from thin air. In fact, thin air can't talk with you. You should, "Be free of all attachments to speech, and be free of all attachments to the mind and its conditions." If you should hear a voice in space talking with you, you should know that it is a demonic state, not something that the "All-encompassing, Perfect, Mirror-like Wisdom" would trifle with. What's the point of doting over your petty little talent? It's totally worthless behavior.

The thoughts of a cultivator must be pure. Don't long for foreknowledge of events. To have this kind of foreknowledge is, in fact, nothing but a lot of trouble, because it leads to discriminations in your thinking and prevents you from being able to concentrate. Being unable to concentrate or focus your energy on cultivation, your idle thoughts run wild, then afflictions come in droves. If you don't crave this foreknowledge in the first place, then you also won't have afflictions, and you are free of impediments. Doesn't it say in the Heart Sutra, "Because there is no impediment, he leaves distorted dream-thinking far behind; ultimately Nirvana!" This, then, is an appropriate goal for a cultivator of the Way.

久參自然會開悟

參到山窮水盡的時候，自然有好消息，
柳暗花明的境界便會出現在眼前。

參禪時，眼觀鼻、鼻觀口、口觀心，這是基本的
法則，可以控制心猿意馬，不令它向外馳求。在
禪堂參禪，不可東張西望，如果前顧後盼，心就
跑到外邊去了，禪就參不下去。這一點，各位要
特別注意！禪七的光陰，非常寶貴，可以說是分
秒必爭，不能空過，要把握時機來參禪，參禪才
能得大智慧。

修道人不要把臭皮囊視為寶貝。沒有這種思想，
才能用功修道；如果有這種思想，就會做它的奴
隸，一天到晚為它服務。所以真正修道的人，將
身體視為臭皮囊，不去重視它；如果重視，則成
為修道的障礙，所謂「借假修真」，只是方便而
已。

在禪堂裏，最大的忌諱，就是在參禪中睡覺。一

Long-term Meditation Will Naturally Bring You to Enlightenment

Keep searching until "the mountains vanish and the rivers disappear." Then spontaneously, the good news will arrive, and you will experience a state "beyond the shadows of the willows and the vivid blossoms."

The basic rule in Chan meditation is: "Let your eyes contemplate your nose; let your nose contemplate your mouth; let your mouth contemplate your mind." This allows us to control the monkey of the mind and rein in the wild horse of our thoughts, so that they stop running outside seeking things. As we sit in the meditation hall, we may not stare left and right, because if we gaze all around, then our mind will wander outside, and we won't be able to investigate Chan. Please pay heed to this point, everyone! The time in a meditation retreat is extremely valuable; you could say that there is not a second to lose. We must seize the time and investigate Chan, because only through this investigation can we attain wisdom.

Cultivators of the Way should not treat their skin-bag of a body as a treasure. Only people who are free of this idea can apply effort in cultivating the Way. If you treat your body as a precious thing, then you will become its slave and serve its whims all day long. Therefore, genuine cultivators treat the body as a "stinking bag of skin" and don't prize it highly. Valuing the body is an obstacle to cultivation. We should merely "borrow the false to cultivate what is true," and see it as just an expedient means.

The biggest taboo in the Chan Hall is sleeping during meditation.

般人參禪，容易犯的兩種毛病：一為掉舉，一為昏沉；不是打妄想，就是打瞌睡。用功的人，聚精會神在參，絕對不會睡覺。若是入定，另當別論。

坐禪可以證得正定正受，也就是三昧。若能證得此境界，便會如如不動，了了常明。如何能證得此境界？就要下一番苦功夫，勇猛精進，心無妄想，到一念不生全體現的時候，就找到本來的面目，本地的風光。

坐禪的關鍵，就在念茲在茲參話頭。所謂「久參自然開悟」，參到山窮水盡的時候，自然有好消息，柳暗花明的境界便會出現在眼前。有人說：「我參加這麼多次禪七，為什麼還不開悟？」因為你不能忍耐一切苦，只想開悟。要知道開悟是從積功累德而來，久而久之，功德圓滿，自然開悟。可是你一點功德也沒有，就想開悟，簡直是癡心妄想，癩蛤蟆想吃天鵝肉，那是辦不到的。

Most meditators have two problems: restlessness and torpor. That is, if they aren't indulging in idle thinking, they'll be dozing off. Those who know how to work hard, however, will be concentrating their energy on their inquiry; they will absolutely not be sleeping. And if they can enter samadhi, then that's another story altogether.

Through meditation, you can attain "proper concentration and proper reception," which is samadhi. If you realize this state, then you will be "Thus, thus, unmoving, understanding and perfectly clear." How can you reach this state? You must put in a period of vigorous effort and rid your mind of idle thoughts. Then, "when not even one thought arises, the entire substance comes into view," and you will discover your original face, your fundamental identity.

The key to meditation is to investigate the meditation topic in thought after thought. A saying goes, "After long-term investigation, you will naturally attain enlightenment." Keep searching until "the mountains vanish and the rivers disappear," and the good news will naturally arrive, and you will experience a state "beyond the shadows of the willows and the vivid blossoms." Someone may say, "I've attended so many retreats; why haven't I become enlightened?" It's because you haven't been able to endure all kinds of suffering with only the wish to become enlightened. You should realize enlightenment comes from the accumulation of merit and virtue. In time, your merit and virtue will become full, and you will naturally attain enlightenment. To wish for enlightenment without creating any merit or virtue is simply vain thinking. As it's said, "A warty frog has no hope of tasting the flesh of the great, white swan." It's simply impossible.

修道不要爭第一

好的給人家，壞的自己留著。

現在參禪的人，盡在皮毛上用功夫，把參禪當做
比賽，來爭第一。你能坐三小時，我就要坐五小
時，勝過你一招。有這種心理作祟，焉能開悟？
就是坐了八萬大劫，也不能明心見性。爲什麼？
因爲你有勝負心。所謂：

> 爭是勝負心，與道相違背；
> 便生四相心，由何得三昧？

這首偈頌，是警惕修道人，不可爭第一。功夫到
家，智慧現前，自然會有人評判你是第一，那才
是眞第一。如果心想第一，有這種勝負心，就與
道相違背了。

修道的人，要像水一樣，有謙卑心，不爭功、不
貪德，好的給人家，壞的自己留著。老子說：

Don't Compete to Be Number One As You Cultivate the Way

Let others have the desirable things, while keeping the undesirable things for yourself.

The participants in our Chan Session are working at a very superficial level. They've turned meditation into a contest to see who'll win first place. They are thinking: "If you meditate for three hours, then I'll meditate for five hours, so that I can keep the upper hand." If you let such thoughts control you, can you really expect to get enlightened? Even if you sat still for eighty thousand great eons, you'd still be unable to understand your mind and see your nature. Why? Because you have thoughts of victory and defeat.

> *Fighting brings an attitude of victory and defeat*
> *That stands in opposition to the Way.*
> *Further, it provokes the four marks,*
> *Which sends samadhi-power far away.*

This verse warns cultivators not to fight to be number one. When your spiritual skill matures and your wisdom appears, other people will spontaneously acclaim you as number one. Then you can be considered truly number one. But if you contend to be first, then your attitude of victory and defeat stands in opposition to the Way.

Cultivators of the Way should be like water, humble and modest, neither contending for merit nor striving for virtue. They bestow

119

上善若水，水善利萬物而不爭。
處眾人之所惡，故幾於道矣。

上善，就是第一流的修行者，如水一般，向低窪之處流去。雖然水對萬物有利益，可是它不爭功德。不論是飛潛動植，或是胎卵溼化，它都一視同仁，供給所需。修道人，亦復如是，對一切眾生，都視爲過去的父母、未來的諸佛，要慈悲爲懷，方便爲門，拯救他們出離苦海。凡是眾人所不願意住的地方，也要去住，有這種的思想，就離道很近了。凡是有勝負心，就不合乎修道的宗旨，就違背了道。

修道人要沒有四相心。「無我相」，誰在修道？修道的人也沒有了。「無人相」，沒有和人比賽的心。「無眾生相」，我相沒有，人相沒有，所以眾生相也空。「無壽者相」，既然眾生相也空了，那來的壽者相？若是有爭強論勝的思想，就有四相心；有了四相心，從什麼地方能得到正定正受？這個道理，不妨琢磨琢磨。一言以蔽之：

advantages on others and keep the disadvantages for themselves. Lao Zi said,

The highest kind of goodness resembles water,
As it benefits all things and never contends.
It stays in places that most people despise,
And thus it approaches the Way.

"The highest goodness" refers to the best kind of cultivators who resemble water as it flows into the lowest places. Although water benefits all things, it refuses to compete for merit and virtue. Whether it is birds, fish, beasts, plants, or creatures born from wombs, eggs, moisture, or transformation, water treats them all with equal kindness and gives them all whatever they need. Cultivators of the Way are just like water, in that they regard all living beings as their parents from lives past and as Buddhas of the future. We make kindness and compassion our duty and expedient resourcefulness our practice as we rescue living beings from the sea of suffering. A cultivator is willing to dwell in places where most living beings are unwilling to stay. With this attitude, he stays close to the Way. Any thoughts of victory and defeat do not accord with the creed of a cultivator and stand in opposition to the Way.

Cultivators of the Way want to be free of the four marks. They want to have no mark of self. Ask yourself: "Who is this here cultivating the Way?" You'll find that there isn't anyone cultivating. They want to have no mark of others; they have no thoughts of competing with others. They want to have no mark of living beings. Since they have no marks of self or others, quite naturally, the mark of living beings is also emptied out. They want to have no mark of a life span: Since the mark of living beings has been emptied out, how could there be any mark of a life span? But once you indulge

121

　　有四相心，即是凡夫；

　　無四相心，即是菩薩。

修道人要記住《金剛經》的四句偈：「一切有爲法。如夢幻泡影。如露亦如電。應作如是觀。」凡是有形有相的，皆是有爲法。有爲法，好像作夢，好像幻化，好像泡沫，好像影子，好像電光，皆是虛妄而無實體。一切的一切，皆應該這樣來觀察，才能明白眞實的道理，就不會執著，不會打妄想了。

在《金剛經》上又說：「過去心不可得。現在心不可得。未來心不可得。」過去心爲什麼不可得？因爲過去已經過去了，還管它做什麼。現在心爲什麼不可得？因爲現在念念不停。你說這是現在，等你說完，現在又過去了，時間不會停留的。未來心爲什麼不可得？因爲還沒有來嘛！你說那是未來，可是它又來了，連未來也沒有。所以過去、現在、未來，三心了不可得。能依佛所說的法去修行，直截了當可達涅槃之境。

修道人要依正知正見的法爲準繩，勇猛修習。這

in thoughts of victory, the four marks will arise. Once they arise, how can you attain "proper concentration and proper reception?" Why don't you try this out in practice? In a word, anyone who maintains the four marks is an ordinary person. But someone who can be free of them is a Bodhisattva.

Cultivators should remember this verse from the *Vajra Sutra*,

> *All things born of conditions are like dreams,*
> *Like illusions, bubbles, and shadows;*
> *Like dewdrops, like flashes of lightning:*
> *Contemplate them in these ways.*

Anything with shape or form is considered a "dharma born of conditions." All things born of conditions are like dreams, illusory transformations, bubbles of foam, and shadows. Like dewdrops and lightning, they are false and unreal. By contemplating everything in this way, we will be able to understand the truth, let go of attachments, and put an end to random thoughts.

The *Vajra Sutra* also says, "Past thoughts cannot be obtained, present thoughts cannot be obtained, and future thoughts cannot be obtained." Why can't we get at past thoughts? Because they've already gone by. What's the point of worrying over them? Why can't we get at present thoughts? Because the present moment doesn't stop for even an instant. If you claim that this moment is the present, as soon as the words leave your mouth, that "present" has already gone by; time never stops. Why do we say that future thoughts cannot be obtained? Because the future hasn't yet arrived. You may admit that it hasn't yet come, but right then it arrives, so the "not-yet-come" (literal Chinese translation for "future") doesn't

時候，「離言說相」，言說的相也沒有了，沒有什麼話可說的。「離心緣相」，心緣的相也沒有了，沒有什麼緣可攀的。「離文字相」，文字的相也沒有了，沒有什麼文字可代表，可說出來。既然說不出來，還有什麼可回憶？還有什麼放不下？還有什麼可認真？各位！要在這個地方用功，不可在皮毛上用功。

有人在想：「今天坐禪，腿不知疼，腰不知痠，不知不覺到開靜的時間。」因為你在睡覺嘛！當然什麼也不知道。不要誤認是境界，若是有這個執著，則容易走火入魔，大上其當。

各位注意！凡是從外來的境界，不要注意它，不要理會它，聽其自然，不隨它轉。在《楞嚴經》上講得非常明白，希望參禪者，要徹底研究「五十陰魔」的來龍去脈。《楞嚴經》是參禪人的寶鑑，所有修道人宜深入鑽研。

exist either. Therefore, the past, the present, and future are three thoughts that cannot possibly be obtained. If we can cultivate according to the Dharma that the Buddha spoke, then straightaway, we can realize the state of Nirvana.

Cultivators of the Way must use proper knowledge and views as their standard and cultivate vigorously. Our goal is to "leave behind the mark of speech," so that there's nothing left to say. We also want to "leave behind the mark of the mind and its conditions," so that there's nothing left to climb on. We want to "leave behind the mark of written words." Once words also are gone, they can't represent our speech at all. Since there's no way to express with words, what is there to remember? What is there that we can't put down? What is left to take so seriously? We should apply ourselves to this, and stop toying with the superficial aspects.

Someone is thinking, "Today in meditation, my legs didn't hurt and my back has stopped aching. Before I knew it, it was time to stand up and walk." That's because you were sleeping! Of course you knew nothing at all! Don't misinterpret this state. If you become attached, then you can easily enter a demonic state and be taken in.

Pay attention to this, everyone! Pay no heed to external states. Ignore them completely. Let states come and go naturally. Don't let them influence you one way or the other. The *Shurangama Sutra* explains this matter quite clearly. I hope that all Chan meditators will look into the details of the Fifty Skandha-demon States of that Sutra very thoroughly. The *Shurangama Sutra* serves as a precious mirror for Chan meditators, and every cultivator of the Way ought to be thoroughly familiar with it.

修道目的爲成佛

修道要有正知正見，不可顚倒是非，
黑白要分清楚。

爲什麼要修道？爲成佛。怎樣能成佛？初步修「
諸惡莫作，眾善奉行。」進一步「勤修戒定慧，
息滅貪瞋癡。」再進一步「發菩提心，行菩薩道
。」所以在未成佛之前，要選擇光明平坦的大道
去行，不可以貪圖方便，去走崎嶇小路，那會迷
失方向。謹之！愼之！

眞正的修行人，依法修持，不怕苦、不怕難，勇
猛前進，直達佛果。所謂：

> 鐵杵磨繡針，
> 功到自然成。

用功用到極點，自然成就佛果。不可標異現奇，
不可自誇其德，有這種思想的人，是永遠都不會
成佛的。

126

Our Goal in Cultivating the Way Is Buddhahood

Cultivation of the Way requires proper knowledge and proper views. You must not confuse right and wrong. You have to distinguish black from white clearly.

Why does a person want to cultivate the Way? Because he wants to become a Buddha. How does one become a Buddha? The first step is to "Avoid doing evil deeds, but respectfully practice all good deeds." The next step is to "Diligently cultivate precepts, concentration, and wisdom; put an end to greed, hatred, and stupidity." The next step is to make the great resolve for Bodhi, and cultivate the Bodhisattva Path. Thus, before one has realized Buddhahood, one must choose the broad, level, great road of light to travel on. We can't plan to get off cheaply by walking the treacherous, narrow bypaths, or else it's easy to lose our direction. Pay heed to this! Take care!

Real cultivators rely on the Dharma in their cultivation. They fear no pain, and they fear no difficulty, but make courageous advance all the way to Buddhahood. A saying goes:

Grind the iron pillar down to sewing-needle size.
Your efforts will bear fruit when the work matures.

Simply apply effort to the ultimate point and you'll naturally accomplish Buddhahood. Don't try to show yourself off as somebody special or unusual, and don't brag about your virtue.

127

開五眼的境界，能見十方諸佛，在那裏怎樣用功修行，怎樣成佛果；能見十方諸菩薩，在那裏怎樣用功修行，怎樣成菩薩果；能見十方諸阿羅漢，在那裏怎樣用功修行，怎樣成阿羅漢果。這些境界，皆一目了然。

開五眼的人，一念之間，能將佛所說的三藏十二部經典，通達明瞭，照了諸法實相。

三皈依的文說：

自皈依佛，當願眾生，體解大道，發無上心。

自皈依法，當願眾生，深入經藏，智慧如海。

自皈依僧，當願眾生，統理大眾，一切無礙。

如能「深入經藏，智慧如海」，這時候，無所不通、無所不明、無所不知、無所不見，這才是大徹大悟。不可因小失大，爲貪圖小境界，而把本有的大圓鏡智遮住了，那就不能深入經藏，不能智慧如海。

People who have such thoughts will never attain Buddhahood.

If you realize a state in which you have use of the Five Spiritual Eyes, then you'll be able to see how all Buddhas throughout the ten directions cultivate to attain Buddhahood. You'll see how all Bodhisattvas of the ten directions cultivate to attain Bodhisattva-hood. And you'll see how all Arhats in the ten directions cultivate to attain Arhatship. States such as these will reveal themselves to you with a single glance.

Someone who has opened the Five Eyes can, in a single instant, thoroughly understand the ultimate reality of all dharmas and comprehend the entire Twelve Divisions and Three Treasuries of the Canon the Buddha spoke.

The verse for taking refuge with the Triple Jewel says:

> *To the Buddha I return and rely,*
> *Vowing that all living beings*
> *Understand the Great Way profoundly,*
> *And bring forth the Bodhi-mind.*

> *To the Dharma I return and rely,*
> *Vowing that all living beings*
> *Deeply enter the Sutra-treasury,*
> *And have wisdom like the sea.*

> *To the Sangha I return and rely,*
> *Vowing that all living beings*
> *Form together a great assembly,*
> *One and all in harmony.*

If one can "deeply enter the Sutra-treasury and have wisdom like the sea," there will be nothing he does not fathom, nothing he does

129

開大智慧的人，絕對不貪小境界。凡是貪小境界的人，乃是不認識真假，把黃金當黃銅，或把黃銅當黃金，甚至於不要鑽石而要玻璃。爲什麼？因爲沒有辨別真假的能力。

修道要有正知正見，不可顛倒是非，黑白要分清楚，不可魚目混珠，不可濫竽充數。否則就是邪知邪見，永不成佛。

什麼是正知正見？淺言之，沒有三毒心，身心就會清淨，智慧就會現前，能照破無明的黑暗，能滅除煩惱的熱病。到這種境界，便證得果位。希望大家向這個目標邁進。

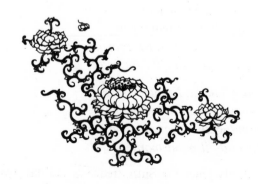

not understand, nothing he does not know, and nothing he does not see; this is great and penetrating enlightenment. Don't miss out on the great because you cling to the small. Don't allow your greed for petty states to obscure the Great, All-encompassing, Mirror-like Wisdom that is inherently yours. If you do, you won't be able to deeply enter the Sutra-treasury and have wisdom like the sea.

People who realize great wisdom definitely would not crave petty states. Someone who is greedy for petty states is someone who does not clearly distinguish truth from falsehood; he mistakes brass for gold and assumes that gold is brass. He would rather have a piece of crystal than a diamond. Why? Because he can't distinguish between true and false.

Cultivation of the Way requires proper knowledge and proper views. You must not confuse right and wrong. You have to distinguish black from white clearly. Avoid mistaking fish-eyes for pearls. Don't march in place just to kill time. Otherwise, you will acquire wrong knowledge and views and will never succeed in cultivation of Buddhahood.

What are proper knowledge and views? Simply put, if we can get rid of the three poisons in our thoughts, then our body and mind will be pure. Wisdom will appear before us, and we'll be able to illuminate right through the darkness of ignorance and put an end to the feverish illness of afflictions. Only at this stage can we attain the positions of sagehood. I hope that all of you will advance towards this goal!

停止你的妄想吧！

怎樣才能不打妄想？
別無二法，就是參話頭。

諸位坐在禪堂裏，表面上在打禪七，可是心裏是在打妄想。這個妄想，忽然而天，忽然而地，忽然而餓鬼，忽然而畜生。這種種的妄想，都離不開貪瞋癡。說是勤修戒定慧，可是不修戒定慧；說是息滅貪瞋癡，可是不息貪瞋癡，就是這樣奇怪。不但一生一世是這樣，而且生生世世都是這樣，所以在六道輪迴中，頭出頭沒永不停止。做狗的時候，覺得是第一；做貓的時候，也覺得是第一；總而言之，無論做什麼眾生，總覺得自己是第一。爲什麼？因爲有無明的執著。如果眞心修道，努力參禪，就能解脫輪迴之苦，證得涅槃之樂。

有的人修行不認眞，隨梆唱影，在禪堂裏混光陰。人家坐我也坐，人家行我也行，人家怎樣我就

Stop Your Idle Thoughts!

How can you be free of these idle thoughts? There is no other method: simply investigate your meditation topic.

Those of you in the meditation hall appear to be taking part in a Chan Session, but your minds are engaging in idle thinking. Your idle thoughts take you suddenly into the heavens and suddenly back to earth. Suddenly you are ghosts, then suddenly you become animals. You produce a profusion of idle thoughts, yet none of them go beyond greed, hatred, and stupidity. You claim to be diligently cultivating precepts, concentration, and wisdom, but in fact you are not cultivating precepts, concentration, and wisdom! You claim to be eliminating greed, hatred, and stupidity, yet you are not eliminating them. That's how strange it is! Not only are you this way in the present life, you are this way in life after life. That's why you rise and sink ceaselessly in the six paths of rebirth. Reincarnated as a dog, we feel we are number one. Reborn as a cat, we also feel we are number one. In general, no matter what type of creature we become, we always consider ourselves to be number one. Why is this? Because we have attachments that arise from our ignorance. If we use a true mind to cultivate the Way and work hard at Chan meditation, then we will be able to liberate ourselves from the suffering of reincarnation and realize the bliss of Nirvana.

Some people don't take their cultivation seriously, but just follow along with the crowd and waste all their time at the retreat. This is

怎樣，把生死的問題，拋到九霄雲外，一點也不認爲重要，不肯眞正用功，不肯決心修道，又不肯把妄想打死。坐在那裏，打一個妄想又一個妄想，沒有停止的時候，一天打了八萬四千個妄想，還覺得不夠。妄想、妄想！被妄想搞得心亂如麻，神魂顛倒，眞是太可憐了！

那麼要怎樣才能不打妄想？別無二法，就是參話頭。話頭雖然也是妄想，可是它能令你的精神集中，不向外馳求。這是以毒攻毒的辦法，用一個妄想來控制多個妄想，將一個妄想參來參去，就沒有妄想。到了沒有妄想的境界，便是開悟的時機，這時候，或一言、或一行、或一舉、或一動，都是開悟的鑰匙。

their attitude: "I just sit when the others sit, and walk when they walk. I just do what everyone else does." Such people take the matter of birth and death and simply throw it out beyond cloud nine. They don't take it at all seriously. These people are neither willing to really apply themselves, nor to dedicate themselves to cultivation. They are unwilling to beat their idle thoughts to death. They simply sit here, endlessly entertaining one idle thought after another. In a single day they may bring up eighty-four thousand idle thoughts, yet they still aren't satisfied. Idle thinking! Idle thinking! They let these idle thoughts tie their mind into knots and turn their spirits upside-down. How pathetic!

How then, can you be free of these idle thoughts? There is no other method: simply investigate your meditation topic. Although the meditation topic is also a idle thought, it can still bring your energy to a concentrated focus and prevent it from running outside. It is the method of "fighting fire with fire"; thus we use one idle thought to counter and control many idle thoughts. When one idle thought is investigated from front to back, one will no longer have idle thoughts. When one reaches the stage of having no idle thoughts, there is a chance for enlightenment to occur. At that time, a single word, a single act, a single gesture, or a single motion can serve as the key that opens the lock to your enlightenment.

入定不是睡覺

入定，好像活死人，但有知覺。

有人問我：「入定和睡覺有什麼不同？」簡而言之，入定的姿勢，仍然端坐，背直如筆，端正不偏，或者呼吸停止，或者脈搏停止，望之，好像活死人，但有知覺。可以坐一天不動，十天不動，甚至一個月不動。睡覺的姿勢，頭歪身斜而不自主，氣出氣入，呼呼有聲，甚至鼻息如雷。不同之處，就在這個地方。

參禪的過程，好像讀書一樣，由小學、中學、大學，然後進研究所，經過這四個階段，才能獲得博士學位。參禪這個法門，亦復如是，分為四個步驟，也就是四禪的境界。簡略述之如下：

初禪名「離生喜樂地」。就是離開眾生的關係，得到另外一種快樂。此非凡夫所得的快樂，而是

Entering Samadhi Is Not the Same as Sleeping

A person in samadhi appears to be dead, but in fact, awareness and feelings still remain.

Someone has asked, "What is the difference between samadhi and sleep?" To put it simply, people who are in samadhi will be sitting in an upright posture with perfectly straight backs, not leaning in any direction. Perhaps their breathing will stop or their pulse will cease, so that they appear to be dead; however, awareness and perception remain. Someone in samadhi can sit for an entire day, for ten days, or even for a month without moving. If a person is asleep, however, his head is usually askew, his body is leaning, and he is not in control of himself. He still breathes, and his breathing may be as noisy as thunder. These are the differences.

The process of Chan meditation is just like that of studying. One proceeds from elementary school to high school, then to college, and then on to graduate school, passing through four stages before one can earn a Ph.D. Likewise, the Dharma-door of Chan meditation is also divided into steps, the Four Stages of Dhyana-concentration, which are briefly explained below:

The First Dhyana is called the Stage of the Happiness Leaving Birth. It takes you beyond what living beings can experience, into a state of happiness beyond what ordinary living beings know. This happiness is found in the spiritual skill of our inherent nature. When you reach the samadhi of the First Dhyana, your breath ceases.

在自性功夫裏邊。到初禪定中，呼吸停止。外邊呼吸停止，內邊呼吸活動起來，好像冬眠一樣的道理。這時，心清如水，明如鏡，照了自性的本體，而知道自己在打坐。

二禪名「定生喜樂地」。在定中，出生一種無比的快樂，所謂「禪悅爲食，法喜充滿。」得到這種快樂，不知道飢餓，所以可以多日不食不飲，沒有關係。但是不可以執著，如果一執著，前功盡棄，就入了魔境，吾人不可不謹慎。二禪的境界，在定中不但呼吸停止，而且脈搏也停止。出定時，又恢復正常。

三禪名爲「離喜妙樂地」。就是離開二禪之歡喜，得到妙不可言的快樂，覺得一切都是佛法，一切都是快樂。三禪的境界，在定中呼吸脈搏停止，意念也停止。這時候，不念善、不念惡，不念是、不念非，也就是一念不生。但不要認爲了不起，這僅是一個過程而已，離了生脫死還有十萬八千里。

四禪名爲「捨念清淨地」。在此境界，連快樂的

Your outer breathing stops and your inner breathing begins to function, just as if you'd entered a state of winter hibernation. Your mind at this time is as pure as water and as clear as a mirror. You can know your fundamental identity and can be aware that you are sitting and meditating.

The Second Dhyana is called the Stage of the Happiness of Producing Samadhi. In a state of concentration, an incomparable happiness comes forth. We refer to it as "taking the bliss of Dhyana as food and being filled with the joy of Dharma." Happiness such as this leaves one unaware of hunger. Thus you can sit for many days without any problem. However, you must not become attached to this state, for as soon as you become attached, all your previous efforts will be wasted and you will enter a demonic state. So you must be extremely careful. At the stage of Second Dhyana, not only does the breath stop, but the pulse stops as well. When one leaves concentration, these processes resume their normal functioning.

The Third Dhyana is known as the Stage of the Wonderful Bliss of Leaving Happiness. One reaches a wonderful, inexpressible happiness that leaves behind the happiness found in the Second Dhyana. You feel that absolutely everything is part of the Buddhadharma, and everything is a source of joy. In this stage, not only do the breath and the pulse stop, but the thinking processes also cease. At this point, you no longer think of good or evil, or right or wrong; not even a single thought arises. All the same, you mustn't feel that such a state is extraordinary. It's simply one step along the way, and it's a million miles away from putting an end to birth and death.

The Fourth Dhyana is known as the Stage of the Purity of

139

念也沒有了，已把它捨棄，而到達清淨無所作為的境界，也就是到了無為而無不為的地步。到了四禪，乃是參禪功夫所必經之路，沒有什麼不得了，不要誤認是證果。如果這樣想，就和無聞比丘犯同樣的錯誤，而墮地獄。

四禪的境界，還是凡夫的地位。如果精進向前，證到「五不還天」的境界，才是證得聖人的地位。但此位尚未了生死，非得超出三界，才能了生脫死。這一點要弄清楚，不可混為一談。

Renouncing Thought. At this stage, not even the thought of happiness remains. You've already done away with it, and you've come to a state of purity in which there's no further action. This is the stage where "There is nothing to do, yet nothing is left undone." The attainment of the Fourth Dhyana is merely necessary part of the process of developing skill in meditation. There is nothing extraordinary about it. Do not mistakenly think that you have already realized the fruition. If you have that idea, you would be making the same mistake as the Unlearned Bhikshu, and you could fall into hells.

One who reaches the level of the Fourth Dhyana is still considered an ordinary person. If he continues to make vigorous progress and realizes the state of the Five Heavens of No Return, only then has he realized sagehood. Even so, he still hasn't put an end to birth and death. One must transcend the Triple Realm before one can end birth and death. This point must be made clear: different stages should not be mixed up.

《楞嚴經》是僞經嗎？

《楞嚴經》無法不備，無機不攝，是一代法門的精髓，成佛作祖之正印。

憨山大師曾經說過這樣的兩句話：「不讀《法華》，不知如來救世之苦心；不讀《楞嚴》，不知修心迷悟之關鍵。」的確是這樣的情形，因爲《楞嚴經》無法不備，無機不攝，乃是一代法門的精髓，成佛作祖之正印。所以參禪打坐的人，必須要熟讀研究這部經，才能明悉「五十種陰魔」的境界，不會上魔王的圈套。否則，境界認識不清，不管什麼境界來臨，就執著它，便容易入魔境，成爲魔王的眷屬。這是一件十分危險的事！

不但〈楞嚴咒〉要背得出來，就是《楞嚴經》也要背熟。所謂「熟能生巧」，到時候便有無窮的受用，有不可思議的感應。凡是研究中國文學的人，《楞嚴經》是必讀之書，因爲此經文辭優美，義理豐富，是一部最理想的經典。

Is the *Shurangama Sutra* an Inauthentic Sutra?

Every dharma is found within the *Shurangama Sutra*, so there are no potentials it fails to attract. It is the essential Dharma for all generations: It is the right seal for becoming a Buddha or a Patriarch.

The Great Master Han Shan (Silly Mountain) once said: "Unless you read the *Lotus Sutra*, you won't know of the pains the Thus Come One took to save the world. Unless you read the *Shurangama Sutra*, you won't know the key to cultivating the mind and awakening from confusion." This says it exactly right, because every dharma that exists is found within the *Shurangama Sutra*, so there are no potentials it fails to attract. It is the essential Dharma for all generations: It is the right seal for becoming a Buddha or a Patriarch. A Chan cultivator must thoroughly master this text and understand the Fifty Skandha-demon States that it explains, in order to escape the snares of the demon-kings. Otherwise, he won't recognize states when they arise, and he will become attached to them and join the retinue of demons. This is extremely dangerous!

We want to be able to recite the Shurangama Mantra from memory, and we also want to memorize the *Shurangama Sutra*. As the saying goes, "Familiarity leads to expertise." When the time comes, we will gain infinite advantages and inconceivable responses. Anyone who studies Chinese literature simply must read the *Shurangama Sutra*. The literary quality of this Sutra is excellent, and its meanings are profound; it is the most perfect Sutra.

有些自命不凡的學者，對於佛學未曾深入研究，
就認為自己是佛學專家、佛學權威，似是而非，
不徹底瞭解佛教的眞諦，亂加批評，貿然提出《
楞嚴經》是僞經的謬論。別有用心的人，就隨聲
附和；這是盲從，實在可憐！

為什麼有人說，《楞嚴經》不是釋迦牟尼佛所說
的法門呢？因為這部經所說的道理太眞實了，把
人的毛病說得太徹底了，令妖魔鬼怪、牛鬼蛇神
，無法橫行，原形畢露。所以他們要故意破壞，
宣傳是僞經，令大家不相信《楞嚴經》，他們才
有生存的機會。如果承認是佛說的法，他們做不
到。第一、對「四種清淨明誨」不能守，第二、
對「二十五聖圓通」的法門不能修，第三、不敢
面對「五十種陰魔」的境界。

如果人人讀《楞嚴經》，明白《楞嚴經》，外道
的神通則失去靈光，毫無效用，使人不再相信他
有神通。所以天魔外道只好妄言破壞，大肆宣傳
，說《楞嚴經》是僞經。

不但在家人這樣誹謗《楞嚴經》是假的，就是出

There are some pretentious scholars who possess no deep understanding of Buddhism and yet consider themselves experts in the field. They see themselves as authorities when they are not. Without a thorough grasp of the principles of Buddhism, they freely criticize the *Shurangama Sutra*, recklessly asserting that it is an inauthentic Sutra. Still others who may be more conscientious, nonetheless, parrot the false claims of the scholars, like the blind following the blind. The situation is truly pathetic!

Why would anybody claim that the *Shurangama Sutra* was not spoken by Shakyamuni Buddha? It's because the principles explained in this Sutra are simply too true. They thoroughly describe people's problems, thus preventing the goblins, demons, "cow-faced ghosts," and "snake-bodied spirits" from running amok and exposing them for what they are. That's why certain individuals defame the Sutra by claiming that it is fraudulent, destroying people's faith in the *Shurangama Sutra* so that they themselves have a chance to survive. If they acknowledged that the Sutra was, in fact, spoken by the Buddha, they would have no way to follow its Dharma. First, they cannot uphold the Four Unalterable Aspects of Purity. Second, they cannot cultivate the Dharma-doors of Perfect Penetration of the Twenty-five Sages. Third, they cannot face the Fifty States of the Skandha-demons.

If everyone reads the *Shurangama Sutra* and understands it, then the spiritual powers of the externalists will lose their magical gleam; they will seem powerless and people will no longer believe that they possess spiritual powers. That's why the celestial demons and externalists have no recourse but to slander the *Shurangama Sutra* and circulate the spurious claim that it is an unauthentic text.

Not only do laypeople slander the *Shurangama Sutra* as false, even

家人也如是云云。爲什麼？因爲一般出家人所受
的教育有限，甚至還有目不識丁的，也看不懂經
典，尤其這部《楞嚴經》，文又深，義又妙，所
以更無法了解，無法辨別眞僞。有人一說某某經
是假的，某某經是僞的，這些人便不加考慮，人
云亦云，所以《楞嚴經》便受到不白之冤。

古時在印度，《楞嚴經》被列爲國寶，禁止運出
國外，凡是出境者，都要嚴格檢查，因爲深恐這
部經流到國外。所以海關對出境的僧人，都特別
注意。

當時（唐朝時代）印度有位高僧，名叫般剌密諦
，他費盡心機，想盡辦法，將《楞嚴經》藏在臂
內，瞞過檢查人員，帶到中國，從廣州登陸。當
時，有一位被武則天所貶的宰相房融，在廣州做
太守，房融於是請般剌密諦法師翻譯這部經，而
他自己爲潤色，此經遂成爲文學的巨著，並獻於
武則天。因爲在當時有《大雲經》僞造的風波，
所以武則天將此經存在宮中，沒有流通。

後來神秀禪師爲國師時，在宮中受供養，有一天

left-home people perpetuate the rumor. Why? Because most left-home people have received limited education; some are even illiterate and cannot understand the Buddhas' Sutras. This is especially the case with the *Shurangama Sutra*: its text is deep, its principles are profound, so many cannot understand it or judge its authenticity. Thus, whenever someone claims that a certain Sutra is unauthentic, these ignorant people simply repeat what they hear without giving it any consideration. This is how the *Shurangama Sutra* has comes to receive its undeserved bad reputation.

In the past, the rulers of India considered the *Shurangama Sutra* a national treasure and forbade its being carried out of India. Travellers were stopped at the borders and thoroughly searched, out of fear that the Sutra would circulate. Sangha members who were leaving the country were especially subject to the scrutiny of the border guards.

In those days (during the Tang Dynasty in China) the eminent monk, Master Paramiti of India, after racking his brains and thinking up every possible means, finally hid the Sutra beneath the skin of his arm to fool the customs inspectors so that it could come to China. He arrived in Canton, and met a Prime Minister named Fang Rong, who had been exiled by the Empress Wu Zetian and was serving as a Magistrate in Canton. Magistrate Fang Rong requested the Venerable Paramiti to translate the Sutra. He himself acted as editor and turned out a masterpiece of literature, which he then presented in offering to the Empress Wu Zetian. Just at that time, China was experiencing a scandal regarding the *Great Cloud Sutra*, a fraudulent text. Empress Wu Zetian concealed the translation in the palace and did not allow it to circulate.

Later, when Dhyana Master Shenxiu was appointed as National

發現此經，神秀大師認爲此經對於禪宗有價值，乃將其流通於世。所以這時，中國才流通《楞嚴經》。據傳說，《楞嚴經》是最後來到中國的經典，但在末法時代，《楞嚴經》最先毀滅，其他經典，則接著漸漸被毀滅，到最後，只剩下一部《阿彌陀經》。

【編按】：宣公上人極力主張《楞嚴經》是千眞萬確的諸佛心印。所以上人來到美國之後，就講《楞嚴經》。爲什麼？因爲佛法傳到美國，擬將末法變成正法。這是上人爲續佛慧命，費的一番心血。茲將《楞嚴經淺釋》，在《萬佛城金剛菩提海》雜誌分期刊出，以供讀者研究，中、英單行本，已出版問世，特此告知讀友。

Master, he sat in the palace to receive offerings. One day he discovered the Sutra, realized its value for meditators in the Chan School, and put it into circulation. Only then did the *Shurangama Sutra* finally become known in China. The *Shurangama Sutra* is said to be the last of the Buddha's Sutras to reach China, but during the Dharma-ending Age, it will be the first Sutra to disappear into oblivion. Following it, the other Sutras will gradually disappear as well, until only the *Amitabha Sutra* will be left.

Note: The Venerable Master Hua endorses the *Shurangama Sutra*'s absolute authenticity, and strongly asserts that it bears, without question, the "mind-seal" of all Buddhas. Upon arriving in America, the first major Sutra he explained was the *Shurangama Sutra*. Why did he choose that Sutra? Because when the Dharma is transmitted to America it transforms the Dharma-ending Age into the Proper Dharma Age. It represents the Venerable Master's lifeblood, given for the purpose of carrying on the Buddha's "wisdom-life." *The Buddhist Monthly—Vajra Bodhi Sea* has been serializing *A Brief Explanation of the Shurangama Sutra* in Chinese and English, and will continue to offer this text to readers.

要修般若波羅蜜多

迴光返照，觀察觀察自己在不在？

「觀自在菩薩。行深般若波羅蜜多時。照見五蘊皆空。度一切苦厄。」這四句是《心經》的精華要理。略釋如下：「觀自在」，是教你迴光返照，觀察觀察自己在不在？自己若在，就不會向外馳求，到處攀緣。若是不在，則容易妄想紛飛，甚至發神經，總要找機會，令人供養。有這種思想，那就不自在。

「菩薩」的行為，一切是利益眾生，以眾生為前提，絕對不是為利益自己。我們凡夫的思想，恰好相反，總想利益自己，而不利益眾生。無論做什麼事，先要計較一番，有利的就做，沒有利的就不做，這就是自私自利的表現。世界為什麼不能和平相處？就因為這種關係。你爭我奪，互不相讓，所以就發生戰爭，造成國破家亡的殘局。

Cultivate the Prajnaparamita (Perfection of Wisdom)!

Look within and contemplate whether or not you're here.

"When the Bodhisattva Avalokiteshvara was cultivating the profound Prajnaparamita, he illuminated the Five Aggregates (Skandhas), saw that they were all empty, and crossed beyond all suffering and difficulty..." This line is the *Heart Sutra*'s essential message, and it can be explained as follows: The Contemplator of Self-Presence (Avalokiteshvara) wants you to reflect inwardly and contemplate whether or not you're here. If you're here, then you won't be seeking outside and exploiting situations. If you are not here, then your idle thoughts will be running wild, to the point that you have a nervous breakdown. You'll always be looking for chances to obtain offerings from people. With such thoughts, you will not be at ease.

In everything a Bodhisattva does, he benefits others. Living beings are his *raison d'etre,* and he would never act for his own benefit. We common people think in exactly the opposite way: we think first of benefiting ourselves and never think of benefiting living beings. In everything we do, we first count up the profits: if the deed is profitable, we go ahead and do it. If it isn't, we don't do it. This is a selfish and self-gratifying attitude. Why can't the world find peace? Precisely because of this attitude. We strive and compete, and refuse to yield to one another. Thus wars break out, and we

151

這位菩薩，他能「行深般若波羅蜜多」，從無始劫以來，一直到現在，生生世世都修深般若法，沒有間斷的時候。修深般若法，（一）沒有驕傲心；若有驕傲心，就是愚癡。（二）沒有自滿心；若有自滿心，就是愚癡。（三）常生慚愧心；不生慚愧心，就是愚癡。（四）不生攀緣心；若生攀緣心，就是愚癡。（五）不生瞋恨心；若生瞋恨心，就是愚癡。（六）不生顛倒心；若生顛倒心，就是愚癡。

我們修道人，以這六種心做爲標準，衡量自己所行所作，是否如法？如法就是智慧，不如法就是愚癡。也就是説，勤修戒定慧，息滅貪瞋癡，就是智慧；不修戒定慧，不滅貪瞋癡，就是愚癡。智慧和愚癡的分別，就在這個地方。

要修深般若，才會照破五蘊中的五十種魔境：在色蘊中有十種陰魔，在受蘊中有十種陰魔，在想蘊中有十種陰魔，在行蘊中有十種陰魔，在識蘊中也有十種陰魔。總括來講，有這五十種；分開來講，有無數無量種，如有不愼，就墮入魔境。總而言之，凡是有邪知邪見的人，都是屬於魔的

witness the tragedy of families being torn apart and nations collapsing.

This Bodhisattva can practice the profound Prajnaparamita. From beginningless time in the past up to this present moment, in life after life, he has practiced the method of Prajna, cultivating it without pause. The first requirement for cultivating profound Prajna is to avoid arrogance. Being arrogant is stupid. Secondly, one must avoid complacency. Being complacent is stupid. The third requisite is to always feel shame and remorse. Not feeling shame and remorse is stupid. The fourth requisite is to avoid exploiting situations. Exploiting situations is stupid. The fifth requisite is to avoid anger and hatred. Feeling anger and hatred are stupid. The sixth requisite is to not be disoriented. Being disoriented is stupid.

Cultivators of the Way make these six requisites their standard in judging to see whether their own behavior accords with the Dharma. If it accords with the Dharma, then that behavior is considered wise. In other words, to diligently cultivate precepts, concentration, and wisdom, and to put an end to greed, hatred, and stupidity is wise behavior. To fail to do this is stupid behavior. The difference between wisdom and stupidity lies right here.

One must cultivate profound Prajna before one can "illuminate and shine through" the fifty states of the skandha-demons found amid the Five Aggregates (skandhas). Ten demonic states appear in each of the Aggregates of Form, Feelings, Thoughts, Activities, and Consciousness. Generally speaking there are fifty states, but when we look into each case separately, there are measureless, innumerable varieties of states. If a cultivator is not careful, he can easily fall into the demons' snares. In general, all people who make use of deviant knowledge and views belong to the retinue of

眷屬；有正知正見的人，都是屬於佛的眷屬。

行深般若波羅蜜多時，才能認清魔的境界，不會
被其動搖。這時候，不但照見五蘊皆空，也度一
切苦厄。五蘊皆空，即是眞空，所謂：

> 眞空無人我，
> 大道無形相。

一切苦厄，就是三災八難之苦厄。

若能將這四句經文的法，修到爐火純青的時候，
就證得八風吹不動的境界。何謂八風？就是稱、
譏、苦、樂、利、衰、毀、譽。這八種風，能把
沒有定力的人，吹得昏頭轉向，不知東西南北。
今將這八風淺釋如下：

（一）稱：就是稱讚。人家稱讚你一聲，覺得
　　　　比吃蜜還甜，心裏很舒服。
（二）譏：就是譏諷。人家諷刺你一句，就受
　　　　不了，心裏就不舒服。
（三）苦：就是苦惱。受一點苦楚，煩惱就起

demons. People with proper knowledge and viewpoints, however, belong to the retinue of Buddhas.

Only when we practice the profound Prajnaparamita can we recognize the demons clearly and not be shaken or influenced by them. When we practice thus, not only can we shine through the Five Aggregates and see how they are all empty, but we also cross beyond all suffering and difficulty. The emptiness of the Five Aggregates is True Emptiness. As a saying goes,

> *True Emptiness is free of self and others;*
> *The great Way is free of shape and features.*

Suffering and difficulty refers to the three disasters and the eight types of difficulties.

If we can cultivate the Dharma in this verse to perfection, we will attain a state in which the Eight Winds cannot affect us. What are the Eight Winds? They are praise, ridicule, pain, pleasure, gain, loss, defamation, and honor. The Eight Winds blow people who lack samadhi-power head over heels, until they cannot tell east from west. Let's look more closely at these eight winds:

1. Praise: This means adulation. When others praise you, it tastes as sweet as honey; it's a comfortable sensation.

2. Ridicule: This means somebody makes fun of you. If someone mocks you, even a little, you can't stand it, and it's a very uncomfortable sensation.

3. Pain: This means suffering. When you experience a little bit of suffering, you become afflicted. Whenever suffering behfalls you, it is a test to see whether or not you can forbear it.

來了；一切苦來折磨你，看你受得了受不
了。

（四）樂：就是快樂。受一點快樂，不要得意
忘形；一切樂都是考驗，看你怎麼辦？

（五）利：就是利益。得到利益就高興，失去
利益就悲哀，這是沒有定力的表現。

（六）衰：就是衰敗。無論遇到什麼艱難，要
損失不計較，失敗不動心。

（七）毀：就是毀謗。有人毀謗你，說你的壞
話，無所謂！應該處之泰然，自然風平
浪靜。

（八）譽：就是榮譽。有人讚歎你，宣傳你的
名望，仍要無動於衷，視功名猶如瓦上
霜。

這八種風，是考驗「心」的法門，在逆境不動心
，在順境也不動心。若是動心，就是修持不夠，
沒有定力的功夫；若是不動心，便證明有功夫。
但是不能自滿，自我宣傳：「八風也吹不動我，
我的定力猶如金剛一般地堅固。」這樣也不對。

4. Pleasure: This refers to happiness. You should not let a little happiness overwhelm you. All kinds of happy states are tests, to see what you will do with them.

5. Gain: This refers to getting advantages. You become pleased when you gain benefits and are sad when you lose them. This shows a lack of samadhi-power.

6. Loss: This refers to failure. No matter what difficulties arise, we ought to take them in stride and not be upset when we lose out.

7. Defamation: This means slander. If someone insults you and spreads tales about you, you shouldn't mind. You should let it pass, come what may. The entire episode will eventually calm down all by itself.

8. Honor: This refers to situations of exaltation. If you are praised by someone and he makes your name known, you should take it in stride and regard glory and honor as no more important than frost on the windowpane at dawn.

The Eight Winds are dharmas that test your mind, to see whether adverse or favorable situations will upset your equilibrium. If they upset you, your cultivation still lacks maturity and you are deficient in the power of samadhi. Someone who remains unmoved by such states has realized genuine skill. Even so, he can't feel complacent and boast "The Eight Winds cannot blow me over, because my samadhi is as solid as Vajra." That is also wrong.

In the Song Dynasty, the layman Su Dongpo was adept in Buddhist study. Although his skill in Chan concentration was immature, he felt himself to be quite accomplished. One day, feeling exuberant and possessed by a sudden inspiration, he penned a verse:

在宋朝有位蘇東坡居士，他對佛學略有研究。雖然他禪定功夫還不夠，卻自覺定力到了相當程度。有一天，心血來潮，靈感忽至，寫了一首偈頌：「稽首天中天，毫光照大千，八風吹不動，端坐紫金蓮。」他以為自己已經開悟，所以請佛印禪師給他印證，於是派遣侍者過江，把偈頌送到金山寺。

老禪師一看，在原紙上寫上：「放屁！放屁！」四個字，交給來人（侍者）帶回。蘇東坡一看，無明火冒三丈高，大發雷霆，豈有此理！這是開悟的偈頌，怎說是放屁？於是過江來找佛印禪師算賬。

不料，來到金山寺的山門時，佛印禪師已在那裏等待他的光臨，就大笑地說：「好一位八風吹不動的蘇大學士，竟被屁風吹過江來，歡迎！歡迎！」（因為他們二人是老道友，時常開玩笑）蘇東坡滿肚子的火，剛要爆炸，被老禪師一說，覺得有理，於是承認自己定力不夠，乃向禪師頂禮謝罪。從此之後，不再說口頭禪了。禪是行的，不是說的，能說不能行，是無有是處的。

I pay my respects to the chief of gods,
Whose hairmark-light illumines the universe;
The Eight Winds blow me not, as I
Meditate on this purple-golden lotus.

He thought he'd already gained enlightenment, and he wanted this enlightenment certified by Chan Master Foyin (Buddha-seal). Thereupon, he sent his servant to Gold Mountain Monastery across the river from his home.

The elderly Chan Master took one look at the verse the messenger handed him and wrote two words on the paper: "Fart! Fart!" and told the attendant to take the message back. Su Dongpo read the reply and blew up in a fit of anger. He thundered, "How dare you! This is my enlightenment testimonial; how dare you call it a fart!?" He promptly rowed across the river to settle accounts with Chan Master Foyin.

Unexpectedly, as soon as he reached the gate of Gold Mountain, Chan Master Foyin was waiting for him, to say "Oh, welcome! Welcome to the Great Adept Su Dongpo, one who is unmoved by the Eight Winds, but who lets a couple of tiny farts blow him all the way across the river. Welcome!" The two were old friends and fellow cultivators, and they were in the habit of joking with each other. Su Dongpo's volcanic anger, right on the verge of exploding, was cooled off completely by the truth of the Chan Master's statement. All he could do was admit that his samadhi still lacked maturity and bow to Master Foyin. He apologized for making a scene, and thereafter he avoided bragging. Chan skill is proven by practice, not by prattle. If you can't practice what you preach, it doesn't count.

修道人不可打妄語

自己做錯事不承認，還替自己辯護，
有這種思想和行爲，焉能修道？

在禪堂裏要循規蹈矩，不能標異現奇，不能自以爲是，而不守禪堂的規矩。要知道禪堂是造聖人（開悟）的處所，不可以破壞道場，令人失去開悟的機會。這一點，凡是參加參禪的人，要特別注意，要嚴守戒律，不可放逸。

參禪的機會是很難得的，千萬不可錯過。現在大家共同來參禪，這是因爲往昔所種下的善根，才有今天的機緣。用功修道的人，遇到打禪七的良好機會，要把握開悟的時機，就是一分一秒的時間也不浪費。不可因爲一時的快樂，而躲懶偷安。這樣會耽誤開悟的機會，又會墮落在三惡道，到時候，後悔也來不及了。所以我說：

> 莫待苦時方學道，
> 三塗都是懶惰人。

Cultivators of the Way Must Not Tell Lies

Don't want to admit mistakes, so we rationalize for ourselves. How can a person who behaves like this cultivate the Way?

Here in the Chan Hall, we must be orderly and well-mannered, we cannot put on airs or try to stand out. We cannot do as we please and defy the regulations of the Hall. Realize that the Chan Hall is a place where sages are created; thus we may not disturb the Way-place and deprive others of their chance at enlightenment. Those of you who are taking part in the Chan Session should pay attention to this point. You must hold the precepts strictly and not be lax.

It's most difficult to get to join in a Chan Session; under no circumstances should we let this chance slip by. All of you have this chance to investigate Chan together only because you planted down good roots many lives ago. Given the opportunity to join in a Chan Session, a hardworking cultivator of the Way will certainly seize the time and won't waste an instant. He'd never let a fleeting moment of pleasure lull him into laziness; if he did, he'd lose his chance to become enlightened and would fall into the Three Evil Destinies. That would certainly bring him regrets, but to no avail. That's why I say:

> *Don't wait till the pain sets in before you*
> *decide to cultivate the Way.*
> *The Three Evil Destinies are full of lazy souls.*

所以要時時在用功，刻刻在精進。在禪堂裏，將話頭放在心上，行也參話頭，坐也參話頭，參來參去，把話頭參透了，就見到本來真面目。為什麼？因為話頭能照破妄想。乃至於上不知有天，下不知有地，中不知有人，哪會有時間去打妄想呢？要曉得妄想就是妄語，對基本的五戒不守，為爭而打妄語，為貪而打妄語，為求而打妄語，為自私而打妄語，為自利而打妄語。打妄語就是騙人，自己做錯事不承認，還替自己辯護，有這種思想和行為，焉能修道？

人為什麼用功不進步？就因為妄語打得太多了。打一句妄語，就有一百個妄想生出起。這時，坐也坐不住，站也站不穩，這是掉舉。不知如何是好，進也不知對不對？退也不知對不對？無所適從，很不如法。

真正修行人，處處守規矩，時時勤精進，絕對不打妄語，不去攀緣。希望大家不要向打妄語的人學，更不要向不守規矩的人學，這樣不但得不到利益，反而受其害。這一點要謹慎，要小心，如果被傳染，後患無窮。

So we should work hard and be vigorous in every moment. In the Chan Hall, hang your meditation topic squarely before your mind's eye, and investigate it both when walking and when sitting. Investigate it back and forth until you penetrate right through it. Then you will see your original identity. Why? Because the meditation topic cuts through all idle thoughts. Keep investigating until "you are unaware of the heavens above, the earth below, and the people in between." At that point, how could you have time for idle thoughts? We should realize that idle thinking is simply false speech. We have failed to observe the five basic precepts: we tell lies when we contend; we tell lies when we are greedy; we tell lies as we seek gratification; we tell lies as we are selfish; we tell lies as we chase personal advantages. Telling lies deceives people; we don't want to admit mistakes, so we rationalize for ourselves. How can a person who behaves like this cultivate the Way?

Why would someone who works hard fail to make progress? It comes from having told too many lies in the past. Once you utter a single lie, it stirs up a hundred idle thoughts. Then when you meditate, you won't be able to sit still, nor will you be able to stand firmly. You'll be restless and at a loss: "Should I advance? Should I retreat?" You'll be in a muddle, totally out of harmony with the Dharma.

Genuine cultivators adhere to the rules in everything they do. They are constantly diligent and would absolutely not tell lies, nor would they ever exploit situations. I hope that you all will not imitate liars and unruly characters. Not only will you fail to benefit from such people, on the contrary, you'll suffer their harm. Be careful, take heed! Once you catch the infection, the results are disastrous.

Real cultivators fear neither suffering nor hardship. They cultivate

真正修行人，不怕苦，不怕難，時刻認真在修行，不爲外來境界動搖其心。

參！參！參！參到水落石出，就是本地風光。

earnestly at all times and don't allow external situations to disturb their minds.

Investigate! Investigate! Investigate until the waters recede and the rocks appear (the truth is brought to light). Then you will see your original appearance.

圖：江逸子居士提供
Picture provided by:
Upasaka Jiang Yizi

修道人要受苦

福不可享盡，享盡就沒有福了；
苦可受盡，受盡則沒有苦。

所謂「受苦是了苦，享福是消福。」我們修道人
爲什麼要修苦行？一天只吃一餐，就爲要了苦的
緣故。苦了了，便是樂。

福，有應享的福和不應享的福。應享的福，是自
己工作所得來的代價，能夠住好房子，穿好衣服
，吃好東西，坐好汽車，可以享受一番。可是，
要知道享完之後，就消福了，而在福報的銀行就
沒有存款了。

不應享的福，就是在本分之外求享受，由僥倖得
來的福。好像強盜，搶人家的錢，自己享受，這
是不講道理的享受，必定會受到法律的制裁。在
福報銀行的户頭就透支了。

166

Cultivators of the Way
Should Undergo Suffering

We should not enjoy our blessings to their end, for if we did, we would have no blessings left. On the other hand, we can endure suffering to its end, for then there will be no more suffering.

A saying goes: "Enduring suffering puts an end to suffering; enjoying blessings exhausts blessings." Why do cultivators of the Way want to cultivate? We eat only one meal each day because we want to end suffering. Happiness remains once suffering is gone.

Blessings come in two varieties: those we should enjoy, and those we shouldn't enjoy. Blessings we should enjoy are those which come as rewards for work we ourselves have done. Such things as living in a nice house, wearing nice clothes, eating good food, and riding in nice cars are blessings we can enjoy. We should recognize, however, that once these blessings have been enjoyed to their fullest, they will be gone, and our bank account of blessings will be all out of capital.

Blessings we should not enjoy includes things gained by seeking beyond one's rightful share: blessings that come through scheming and trickery, such as money stolen from others. If we enjoy such blessings, then it's unrighteous pleasure, and the law will punish us. We will have overdrawn our bank account of blessings.

Once we enjoy all the blessings that are rightfully ours, our blessings will be used up. How much more is it so with blessings

應享的福，享完之後，福就消了，何況不應享的福，硬要勉強享受，這不但消福，而且還要虧本。因爲這種關係，所以福不可享盡，享盡就沒有福了；苦可受盡，受盡則沒有苦。我們做人要明白這種道理。在困難的環境中，歡喜接受逆境，這樣便無怨恨，也沒有不滿現實的心在作祟。

研究佛法的人，其思想和行爲，與世俗人正好相反。世俗人是順著生死去造業，修道人是逆著生死來消業。無論在什麼境界上，處之泰然，心安理得，便不覺得苦。所謂「吃得苦中苦，方爲人上人」，這是至理名言。

現在講一個受苦的公案，做爲參考。明朝最後一位皇帝，名叫崇禎。他雖有皇帝的智慧，可是沒有皇帝的福報。爲什麼？因爲他的苦沒有受盡。他前生是個沙彌，因爲未到受具足戒的時候，就死了，所以還是個小沙彌。他做沙彌的時候，凡是搬柴運水的苦工，都由他來做，任勞任怨，天天做苦工，來護持道場。

that are not rightfully ours? Should we demand to enjoy those as well? Not only will we burn up our blessings that way, we'll even go bankrupt. For that reason, we should not enjoy our blessings to their end, or else, we will have no blessings left. On the other hand, we can endure suffering to its end, for then there will be no more suffering. We should understand this principle, so that when we find ourselves in distressing circumstances, we happily accept the discomfort. In this way, we avoid all resentment and we don't become dissatisfied or discontent.

The thinking and behavior of people who study Buddhism is exactly the opposite of worldly people. Ordinary worldly people flow with birth and death as they create more karma. Cultivators of the Way oppose the flow of birth and death as they wipe out their karma. No matter what situations arise, they calmly endure them, resting securely in their knowledge of the principles; thus suffering does not seem painful to them. A saying goes, "Only one who has tasted bitterness to the ultimate degree can become an extraordinary person." How true it is!

I'll now tell you a story of one who endured suffering. The last Emperor of the Ming Dynasty was known as Congzhen ("Noble Portent"). Although he possessed the wisdom of an emperor, he lacked the blessings that an emperor needs. Why was this? Because his suffering had not come to an end. In an former life, he had been a novice monk, but he died before receiving complete ordination as a Bhikshu. Thus he remained a Shramanera (novice). As a novice monk, he had to perform all the menial jobs, such as gathering wood and toting water. He simply endured the toil and swallowed his resentment. Every day he engaged in these strenuous chores in service to the monastery.

有一天，他到房頂修理屋瓦，不愼失足，墜地而死。師兄弟就去報告方丈和尚。老和尚知道前因後果，想成就小沙彌，替他了苦，於是乎，對大家宣布：「這個小沙彌做事不小心跌死，對道場有很大的損失。因為他犯了侵損常住的過錯，要懲罰他。你們用馬把他的屍體拖散為止，免得買棺材埋葬。」大家一聽方丈的話，不以為然，師兄弟們發惻隱之心，不聽方丈的命令，因為不忍心這樣去做。他們於是共議：「我們是師兄弟，同修一場，應該把他安葬，不可以用馬拖屍。」大家就出錢買棺材，把他安葬在荒山中。

這個小沙彌因為替廟做苦工，積有功德，來生為人，做了皇帝，身為崇禎。可是只做了十六年的窮皇帝，他在位的時候，天下大亂，內有李自成造反，外有清兵侵境，從來沒有過一天好日子，都是在憂患煎迫中度日。這就是被好心的師兄弟害了，使他的苦未能了盡。如果他們當時聽方丈的話，用馬來拖屍，苦便了了，不會害得崇禎在煤山自縊，而為國殉難。

One day, he climbed onto the roof of a building to patch tiles, carelessly slipped off, and fell to his death. His Dharma-brothers reported the mishap to the Abbot. Knowing the prior causes and later consequences involved, the Abbot wished to bring the novice to accomplishment and end his suffering. Thereupon, he announced publicly, "This novice was not cautious while working, and he fell to his death. He caused this Way-place a major loss. For this offense of incurring loss to the monastery, he deserves serious punishment. Tie his dead body behind a team of horses and drag him around until he is pulled to pieces! This way we can avoid the cost of buying him a coffin." When the monks heard the Abbot's pronouncement, they simply couldn't carry it out. They pitited their Dharma-brother and decided to disobey the Abbot's order, because they couldn't bear to treat the dead one in such a harsh manner. They talked it over: "We are all brothers, fellow cultivators in the monastery, and by rights we should bury him; don't let horses drag his corpse to bits." Then they chipped in contributions to buy the novice a coffin, and buried him out on the mountainside.

Since the young novice had amassed great merit and virtue by doing menial labor for the monastery, he was able to be reborn as a human, as the Emperor Congzhen, in fact. But his reign lasted only sixteen years and was characterized by disaster. While he ruled, China experienced great chaos; Li Zicheng staged his revolt, and the Qing Dynasty armies invaded from abroad. Not knowing a single day of peace, he passed sixteen years in continuous worry and torment. This was because his well-meaning fellow monks had actually harmed him by not allowing him to endure his suffering to the end. Had they followed the Abbot's instructions and dragged his corpse behind horses, his suffering would have been finished then and there, and Emperor Congzhen would not have been forced to commit suicide on Mei Mountain as a national martyr.

171

去妄心存真心

心要正大光明，方能照破一切黑暗。

《華嚴經》上說：

> 若人欲了知。三世一切佛。
> 應觀法界性。一切唯心造。

你行佛心，就是佛；你行菩薩心，就是菩薩；你行緣覺心，就是緣覺；你行聲聞心，就是聲聞；你行天人心，就是天人；你行人心，就是人；你行阿修羅心，就是阿修羅；你行畜生心，就是畜生；你行餓鬼心，就是餓鬼；你行地獄心，就是地獄。

所謂「十法界不離一念心」，由此可知，一切的一切，都是由心所造出來的。有一首關於「心」的偈頌，說得很有道理：

172

Get Rid of False Thoughts; Hold on to True Thoughts

**When your mind is proper, great, and bright,
you can shine right through all the darkness!**

The *Flower Adornment Sutra* says,

> *If someone wants to understand
> All Buddhas of the three periods of time,
> Simply contemplate the nature of the Dharma Realm:
> Everything is made from the mind alone.*

If you put the Buddha's thoughts into action, you're a Buddha. If you practice according to thoughts of a Bodhisattva, you're a Bodhisattva. If you put the thoughts of Those Enlightened to Conditions into practice, you are One Enlightened to Conditions. If you put Hearers' thoughts into practice, you are a Hearer. If you think the way gods do, you're a god. If you have thoughts typical of humans, you're a human being. If you think like asuras, you're an asura. If you have the thinking of an animal, you're simply an animal. If you think the way a hungry ghost thinks, you are a hungry ghost. And if you think the way hell-dwellers do, you are a hell-dweller.

So it is said, "The Ten Dharma Realms are not apart from a single thought of the mind." From this, we can know that absolutely everything is made from the mind alone. There is a verse that

> 三點如星佈，彎鈎似月牙；
> 披毛從斯起，作佛也由它。

仔細研究，這說得很恰當。人在世上，要存正心，不可存邪心。什麼是正心？就是菩提心、平等心、大慈心、大悲心、憐愍心、布施心、慚愧心。什麼是邪心？就是自私心、自利心、嫉妒心、怨恨心、驕傲心、妄想心。我們修道的目的，就是去妄心存眞心，也就是除邪心生正心。

我們一舉一動，若存正念，就是正知正見；存邪念，就是邪知邪見。有邪念的人，以是爲非，以非爲是，將黑作白，將白作黑，顚倒是非，黑白不分。他所作所爲，自己認爲是對的，結果造成罪業，要墮地獄，自己還不知道。因爲這樣，所以諸佛苦口婆心來規勸，不怕麻煩一次又一次地叮嚀：「不要走錯路！不要誤入歧途！」也就是告訴我們修道人，在道場中不可造惡業。所謂：

> 毋以善小而不爲，
> 毋以惡小而爲之。

discusses the mind quite well:

> *Three dots like a cluster of stars,*
> *And a hook shaped like a crescent moon;*
> *Furry creatures come from the mind;*
> *All Buddhas arise from it, too.*

Look into the verse in detail, and you'll find it describes the mind perfectly. We people here in the world should preserve proper thoughts and not cling to deviant thoughts. What thoughts are considered proper? Thoughts of great kindness, great compassion, sympathy, charity, shame, and remorse are truly proper thoughts. What are considered deviant thoughts? Selfish thoughts, thoughts of benefiting oneself, thoughts of jealousy, hatred, pride, and idle thoughts. Our goal as we cultivate is to get rid of false thoughts while preserving true thoughts. In other words, we want to banish deviant thoughts and foster proper thoughts.

We must preserve a proper attitude in every thing we do. These thoughts are proper knowledge and viewpoints. Don't cling to crooked thoughts, or deviant knowledge and viewpoints. A person with deviant views mixes up right and wrong and doesn't distinguish between black and white. He assumes his actions are correct, and so creates evil karma and falls into the hells without knowing why. Therefore, all the Buddhas spare no pains to warn us over and over: "Don't take the wrong turn in the road. Avoid going down dead-end paths!" They want to tell all of us who cultivate the Way not make bad karma in the Way-place. That is to say,

> *Don't assume a good deed is too small to do,*
> *and fail to do it.*
> *Don't assume an evil deed is too insignificant to matter,*
> *and go do it.*

時時要戰戰兢兢，深省警覺，如臨深淵，如履薄冰，來改善自己的習氣毛病，改善自己的惡劣行為，改善自己的聰明鬼、伶俐蟲。要把自己弄清楚，不可糊糊塗塗混日子，以盲引盲，互相欺騙，搞得世界烏煙瘴氣，令世界一天比一天危險，最後成了世界的末日，同歸於盡。

有正念的人，能引導世界的人，走向正大光明之路。人人有同情心，人人有互助心，你幫助我，我援助你，大家互相幫忙。所謂「助人為快樂之本」，又可以說：「為善最樂」，你發善心做善事，這種快樂，無言可以形容，只有行善者，才能體會其中意味。各位不妨試試行善事的滋味如何？它有妙不可言的樂趣。千萬不要走黑暗彎曲的路，不但自己會有失足之憂，也會引人誤入歧途。所以心要正大光明，方能照破一切黑暗。

We should act with caution at all times and take great care. As we get rid of our bad habits and faults and reform our bad behavior, we should be "as if standing near the edge of a deep abyss; or as if treading on thin ice." We should reform in particular our habit of relying on our excuse-maker: the clever, rationalizing "smart-bugs." Take stock of yourself; see yourself clearly. Don't simply pass the days in confusion, blindly following blind men, cheating each other as you go. This attitude has brought the world to its present state of utter, murky chaos, so it grows more dangerous with each passing moment, leading us inevitably on to doomsday and the extinction of the human race.

People who possess proper thoughts are able to guide the citizens of the world onto proper, broad, well-lit roads. On these right roads, everyone shares similar feelings; everyone helps each other along. It's said, "Helping others is the well-spring of joy." Another adage says, "The greatest joy comes from action done for goodness' sake alone." There are no words to fully describe the happiness that results from a good-hearted resolve to do deeds that are purely good. Only someone who actually does such good deeds knows the flavor of this happiness. Do you want to sample a taste of good deeds? It's truly wonderful, joyful beyond description. By no means should you walk down dark and twisting side roads. Not only can you trip and fall on those crooked paths, but you can easily lead others to the same dead end. Only when your mind is proper, great, and bright can you shine right through all the darkness!

迷時師度，悟時自度

要相信自己的智慧，不要相信自己的
愚癡，這一點是非常重要的。

現在是打禪七（一九七七年十二月十五日）的時
間，諸位時時刻刻要提起話頭，去參禪，去用功
。修道人要自己修行，不要依賴他人，更不要依
賴師父。我們是打禪七，不是打師父七，這一點
要弄清楚。有人這樣想：「師父在萬佛聖城的時
候，我就用功修行；師父離開萬佛聖城，我就不
認眞修行。」這種思想，實在要不得。無論師父
在不在萬佛聖城，都要勇猛精進地修行，貫徹始
終，才有成就。否則盡做表面的工作，那是自欺
欺人的行爲，永遠得不到解脫。

參話頭就是參「念佛是誰？」念佛是誰？這要參
是哪一個？說是：「我在念佛。」那麼我死了，
這個「我」又跑到什麼地方去？根本那不是「我
」。這樣說來，那是沒有「我」了。既然沒有「

178

Confused, You Are Saved by a Teacher. Awakened, You Save Yourself.

You should trust in your own wisdom, not your own stupidity. This is a very important distinction!

Now we are holding a Chan Session (December 15, 1977), and you should all be bringing up your meditation topic at every moment, as you investigate Chan and work at meditation. Cultivators of the Way practice on their own; they do not rely on other people, and even less should they rely on their teacher. We are holding a meditation retreat, not a "Teacher-retreat." Please be clear about this point. Someone is thinking: "The Venerable Master is here now at the City of Ten Thousand Buddhas, so I'll take my cultivation seriously. Once he leaves, however, I won't have to cultivate hard anymore." You should not think this way. Whether or not your teacher is at the City, you should cultivate with vigor. Finish what you've started, applying yourself with equal energy all the way through; only then can you succeed. Otherwise your work will always be superficial; you'll only be fooling yourself and fooling others, and you'll never get liberated.

Investigating the meditation topic means asking, "Who is reciting the Buddha's name?" Look into it! Who is it? If you say, "I'm reciting!" then after you die, where has that "I" gone to? In fact, the reciter isn't "I" after all. As we investigate it, there is no "I" to be found. Since there's no "I," then while I'm still alive, there's no need to cultivate, is there? This is a case of incorrect thinking. How

179

我」，那麼還活著的時候，就不需要修行了？這是不正確的想法。應該怎樣呢？就是要參本來的面目，父母未生以前的面目是什麼樣子？參明白了，就可開悟。

念佛是哪一個？時時刻刻在追究，分分秒秒不放鬆。其實用這種功夫，就是以毒攻毒的方法。念佛是誰？雖然也是一個念，但是用一念控制一切念，用這個妄想停止一切妄想。制止到了極點的時候，水落石出，真相大白，便能開悟。

什麼是開悟？就是真真實實認識自己是怎麼回事，證得空理，知道一切是虛妄，這是真知道。知道「本來無一物，何處惹塵埃」這種的境界，也就是明心見性的境界。所謂「明心無難事，見性不知愁」，明心的人，什麼也不愁，所謂：

　　　　自古神仙無別法，
　　　　廣生歡喜不生愁。

這是修道人的座右銘。

should we think then? We should investigate our basic identity. Who were we before our parents bore us? What did we look like then? When you understand the answer to that question, you can get enlightened.

"Who is reciting the Buddha's name?" Pursue this question ceaselessly. Don't let up on it even for a moment. In fact, this technique is a way to use poison to counteract poison. Although the question, "Who is reciting the Buddha's name?" is also a thought, we use one thought to control all other thoughts. One idle thought puts a stop to all idle thoughts. When those thoughts have been brought to an ultimate end, "the tide recedes and the rocks show through." We clearly perceive the true appearance of things, and then we can get enlightened.

What does it mean to get enlightened? It means you truly recognize what you're all about. You realize the principle of emptiness and you know that all things are false. This is truly knowing. You know the state called, "Originally there was not a single thing. Where could dust alight?" It's also called: "Understanding the mind and seeing the nature." It's said that, When you understand the mind, nothing is difficult any more. When you see the nature, all worries are gone. People who understand the mind don't worry about anything. As it is said:

The spirits and immortals of old had no special tricks;
They were simply happy as could be, and they never worried.

This should be the benchmark of all cultivators of the Way.

181

修道人，無論遇到順或逆的境界，皆不動心。若能有這樣的定力，那就不會被境界所轉，而能轉境界，這才是修道人的眞功夫。所謂

　　泰山崩前而不驚，
　　美色當前而不動。

男人見到西施那樣美的女人，當做骷髏觀，自然不動其心；女人見到潘安那樣英俊的男人，當做白骨觀，自然不動其心。否則，見到美女或俊男，就心猿意馬，七上八下，不知如何是好！若是這樣沒有定力，那就會失去道業，這是多麼可惜！

今天我們聽了三步一拜兩位行者的來信，曉得他們有這樣不可思議的境界，有護法善神的保佑。所謂「感應道交」，他們誠心地拜，眞心地念，於是乎感動了天龍八部，時刻在他們的身邊，處處逢凶化吉，遇難呈祥。我們要將他們兩位做爲借鏡，照照自己是怎麼回事？要迴光返照，看看自己是不是這樣地清淨？這樣地光明？這樣有智慧？這樣不打妄想？

Cultivators do not get upset no matter whether they encounter smooth or troublesome situations. With this kind of samadhi-power, instead of being influenced by circumstances, they can influence states. This is the true skill of a cultivator of the Way.

> *If Mount Tai were to collapse before them,*
> *it wouldn't make them blink.*
> *If a ravishing beauty were to pass before them,*
> *they wouldn't be affected in the slightest.*

If you are a man and you see a woman as beautiful as the legendary maiden Xi Shi, simply use "the contemplation of a skeleton" to view her, and naturally your mind will hold steady. If you are a woman and you see a man as handsome as the famous hero Pan An, use the "bare-bones contemplation" to view him, and very naturally, your mind will hold steady. Otherwise, the sight of a beautiful young woman or a handsome young man will turn you upside-down. The monkey-mind and stallion-instinct will run away with you, until you won't know how to cope with it. If you lack samadhi-power to this extent, you will lose ground in cultivation. What a pity!

Today we read a letter from the monks on the bowing pilgrimage, and know that they've experienced some inconceivable states in which Dharma-protecting spirits have come to protect them. This is called "a response in the Way." Because they've been bowing and reciting sincerely, they've moved the gods, dragons, and the rest of the eight divisions to stay constantly at their side. Therefore, no matter what trouble comes up, it always turns out smoothly. We should take their example to reflect upon ourselves: has this happened to us? We should reflect within to see if we have this kind of purity, light, wisdom, and lack of idle thinking.

各位！聽經聞法，要自性自悟，自悟自度。不要依賴師父！要依賴自己，所謂「師父領進門，修行在個人。」要相信自己的智慧，不要相信自己的愚癡，這一點是非常重要的。我們打禪七的目的，就是自性自度。六祖大師曾經說過：「迷時師度，悟時自度。」

我們現在參禪，應該分秒必爭，不可把寶貴的時光空過。所以在打禪七的時間，佛也不拜，過堂也不念供。爲什麼？就是給大家專一用功的機會。多一分鐘參禪，便多一分鐘開悟。哪有時間去打閒岔、去充殼子、去開小會？若三三五五，講是講非，講些無意義的話，把開悟的時光輕易放過，尚不自知，這樣參禪，就是參八萬大劫，也沒有希望。在打禪七的期間，一定要老老實實去參！參「念佛是誰？」參「父母未生以前的本來面目？」這是開智慧的鑰匙。

All of you! As we hear the Sutras and the Dharma, we should awaken in our own nature and, having awakened, take ourselves across. Don't rely upon your teacher. Rely on yourself instead! As it's said, "The teacher leads you to the door, but cultivation depends on the individual." You should trust in your own wisdom, not your own stupidity. This is a very important distinction! The purpose of holding a meditation retreat is to let your nature take itself across. The Great Master the Sixth Patriarch once said,

> When one is still confused, his teacher saves him.
> After one is awakened, he saves himself.

We are now investigating Chan, and we should make the most of every minute. Don't let the precious time pass by in vain. Thus, when we hold our Chan Session, we neither bow to the Buddhas nor perform the meal offering ceremony. Why not? It's to give everyone a chance to concentrate single-mindedly on his meditation. One minute longer of meditation brings one minute more of enlightenment. Who can find time to interrupt the work, or to shoot the breeze, or to gather a small meeting? If you stand around shooting the bull, gossiping over trivia, talking lots of nonsense, then you'll carelessly waste time in which you could be getting enlightened, and you won't even realize it. Meditating in this way, you can investigate for 80,000 great eons, but you have no hope of success. While holding a retreat, you certainly must do honest work and really look into the matter. Which matter? Investigate, "Who is mindful of the Buddha?" Investigate, "What was my basic identity before my parents gave birth to me?" These are the keys to enlightenment.

參禪要克服痛關

我們是來這裏參禪，不是來混光陰的。

今天是新年，我祝各位新年快樂。本來這是世間
的風俗，我們出世的人，不應該再有這種習氣。
可是要知道我們大家還在這個世界上，如果和世
間距離太遠，那麼和人的距離也遠了。所以還是
依世俗之禮，向你們說一句「新年快樂」。那麼
我再對你們說一首偈頌：

今逢一九八二年，十方聚會來參禪；
迴光返照觀自在，萬佛城中選聖賢。

新年是快樂，我們參禪應該得到禪悅爲食，以參
禪做爲飲食。眞正參禪的人，吃飯或未吃飯？忘
了。穿衣服或未穿衣服？忘了。睡覺或未睡覺？
忘了。參到極點處，上不知有天，下不知有地，
中不知有人，和虛空合成一體，到無人、無我、
無眾生、無壽者的境界。既然是這樣子，那麼腿

In Chan Meditation, We Must Pass Through the Gate of Pain

We have come here to practice Chan, not to fritter time away.

Today is New Year's Day, and I bid all of you a Happy New Year. This is, in fact, a worldly sentiment and we who seek to realize world-transcending wisdom should not dwell on such mundane habits. Nonetheless, we should recognize that we are still part of this world, and if we leave the mundane world too far behind, we'll also be leaving people too far behind. That's why I invoked a bit of standard etiquette to give you all my greeting: Happy New Year! I'd also like to recite a verse:

> *The year 1982 is now close at hand;*
> *All ten directions' cultivators come to practice Chan.*
> *Reverse the light and introspect: contemplate at ease.*
> *At the City of Ten Thousand Buddhas, we will choose*
> *sages and worthies.*

Since the New Year brings happiness, we can all realize the state of "taking the bliss of Chan as our food," and let our sustenance come from Chan meditation. A person who is genuinely doing the work of Chan has forgotten whether or not he has eaten. He has forgotten whether or not he got dressed. He has forgotten whether or not he slept. When one investigates to the ultimate point, he is no longer aware of heaven above, earth below, or people in between. He has merged completely with empty space. He no longer has any sense

痛也不怕痛了，腰痠也不怕痠了，一切一切都要用忍耐的功夫來忍受著。既無人、無我、無眾生、無壽者，那又有誰在痛呢？尤其是這種痛要過關，痛過去就不知痛。如果過不了關，便總是在痛中；若過了關，不但不知痛，而且非常自在，非常快樂。

「參禪」這一法門，沒有再比它更妙的，能得到禪悅為食，法喜充滿的境界。因為這個緣故，所以古來參禪的人，可以連坐幾天，不起於座。那麼他的腿痛不痛？當然痛啊！可是他能忍受，能忍人所不能忍的，受人所不能受的。他有一種勇猛精進的力量，只知向前進，不知向後退，所以才有成就。

參禪要有忍耐心，那是開悟的本錢。好像做生意一樣，有了本錢，生意才能發展，才有希望賺大錢。我們參禪，要克服痛關；通過痛關，過了關之後，光明大道就在眼前，直達明心見性的境界。沒有過關時，就好像「山窮水盡疑無路」的境界；過了關，好像「柳暗花明又一村」的境界。

of self, others, living beings, or a life span. In this state he fears neither the pain in his legs nor the ache in his back. No matter what comes up, he uses the skill of patience to endure it. Since he has no sense of self, others, living beings, or a life span, who remains to feel pain? Once you pass through the gate of pain, you are no longer aware of any pain. If you don't pass the gate, however, then the pain is still there. If you pass through the gate, then not only does the pain stop, but you also feel very carefree and happy.

The Dharma-door of Chan meditation has no rival in its wondrousness; one attains the state of "taking Chan bliss for food, and being filled with the joy of Dharma." This is the way Chan meditators in ages past could sit for days on end without leaving their benches. Do you suppose their legs hurt? Of course they hurt! But they were able to endure the pain; they could tolerate what others found intolerable; they could endure what others found unendurable. They had the strength and vigorous courage to only advance and never retreat; this is how they succeeded in cultivation.

Chan meditation requires patience; patience is the basic capital of your enlightenment. For example, when we go into business, we need some capital. Only then can our business expand; only then can we hope to earn money. In Chan meditation, we must make it through the gate of pain. Penetrating this gate comes first. Once we're through, a brightly-lit road appears before us, and we travel on it straight ahead to the state where we can "understand our mind and see our nature." Before we pass through the gate, we are in a state where "the mountains have ended, the rivers have vanished, and we doubt there is a road ahead." But then once you pass the gate, your state becomes like "another village appearing, there beyond the bright flowers and shadowy willows."

捨不了死，換不了生；
捨不了假，成不了眞；
捨不了苦，得不了樂。

我們參禪，要有這樣的精神，才能有所成功。要把困苦艱難的關打破，然後才能得到另外一種境界。因爲這個緣故，所以我們要專一其心來參禪。各位注意！我們是來這裏參禪，而不是來這裏混光陰的，要拿出眞正的志願來參，拿出眞正的忍耐來坐。要知道世間的事，沒有不勞而獲的，沒有出力，而想得到代價，哪有這樣容易的事？那是癡人妄想，不可能的事。非得拿出眞正的力量來，才能有所成就。新年大家都有新希望，希望今年開悟，希望大家向這個目標邁進，若不到開悟的境界，不停止參禪。

一九八二年禪七 一月一日至八日
開示於萬佛聖城萬佛寶殿

190

If I can't renounce death, I'll never gain life.
If I can't renounce what's false, I'll never gain what's true.
If I can't let go of suffering, I'll never attain happiness.

We must use this kind of spirit in our investigation of Chan if we want to have any accomplishment.We have to smash through the gate of trouble and difficulty before we can attain another state of reality. This is why we must concentrate our minds as we meditate. Please pay attention! We have come here to practice Chan, not to fritter time away. Apply yourself to the investigation with genuine determination and true forbearance. We know that nothing in the world comes easily; how can you expect something in return for nothing? Only fools think that way; only they dream such impractical dreams. The only way to success is through your own efforts. We all bring forth our brand-new aspirations at the New Year, hoping to get enlightened, perhaps. Let's all make that our goal ahead, and not stop meditating until we actually reach the enlightened state!

A talk given during a Chan Session from January 1–8, 1982,
The Hall of Ten Thousand Buddhas, The City of Ten Thousand Buddhas

怎樣才夠資格參禪？

不願做的事，要忍耐去做；
受不了的苦，要忍耐去受。

無論做什麼事情，都要經過一番的鍛鍊，然後才
會成功。參禪的法門，更不容易，要受多方面的
辛苦和鍛鍊，才能上路。凡是打禪七的人，最重
要的要有忍耐心；自己不願做的事，要忍耐去做
；受不了的苦，要忍耐去受。要有這種精神，才
夠資格參禪，否則一切免談。身在禪堂內，心在
禪堂外，參到何時，亦是枉然，無有成就可言。

參禪就是要鍛鍊金剛不壞身，既然心甘情願來受
鍛鍊，那麼能受得了苦，更應該去受，所謂

受苦是了苦，享福是消福。

我們歡喜做的事情，更要努力去做，不要辜負了
來打禪七的初衷。這一點，各位要特別注意。

What Makes One Qualified to Practice Chan Meditation?

You must patiently put up with the tasks you dislike doing. Trials you find unbearable must be borne anyway.

No matter what we do in the world, we can only hope for success after undergoing a period of smelting and refining. Practicing the Dharma-door of Chan meditation is even more difficult. We can make headway only after enduring toil and discipline in every way. Patience is the single most important requisite for meditators. You must patiently put up with the tasks you dislike doing. Unbearable suffering must be patiently endured. With this kind of spirit, you are qualified to practice Chan meditation. If you cannot be this patient, then there's nothing more to say. If your body is sitting in the hall, but your mind is out roaming far beyond the hall, your efforts will be entirely fruitless; you won't achieve any success.

The purpose of investigating Chan is to smelt a Vajra-indestructible body. Since you have your heart set on smelting a Vajra-body, you should go ahead and endure as much suffering as you can put up with. Because, as the saying goes,

> *Enduring suffering ends suffering;*
> *Enjoying blessings uses up blessings.*

As for the things we like to do, we should do them with even more alacrity, and not fail to fulfill the intent that brought us to the Chan Hall in the first place. Everyone should take note of this!

一身病苦從何來？

生怪病的人，在過去生中，
多數貪便宜，不肯吃虧。

法界佛教總會所屬法界佛教大學，這次組織亞洲
區訪問團，到東南亞弘揚佛法。在未起程之前，
我便知道會有種種的障礙，因爲我到什麼地方弘
法，一定會被人所嫉妒和障礙。爲什麼？因爲我
太直，不會同流合污，所以遭人嫉妒。可是我有
把握，邪不勝正，牛鬼蛇神，無能爲患。

我有信心，佛菩薩時時護我的法。我所到之處，
雖然遇到很大的障礙，可是不起作用，不會發生
意外的問題，處處逢凶化吉，平安無事，這是蒙
佛菩薩的加持。

我所到的地方，每天都有很多患病的人，來求醫
治。凡是患病的人，皆因業障深重；若是沒有業
障，則不會生怪病。凡是來見我的人，都是生奇

Where Do Illnesses Originat

For the most part, these people with strange illnesses had sought "bargains" in their past lives and had been unwilling to take a loss.

Dharma Realm Buddhist University, under the auspices of the Dharma Realm Buddhist Association, organized a tour of Southeast Asia to spread the Buddhadharma. Before we set out on the journey, I was aware that we would face a variety of obstacles, because wherever I go to propagate Dharma, I always encounter jealousy. Why is that so? Because I am too straightforward; I've never been able to just flow along with the crowd. As a result, I run into others' jealousy. However, I have confidence, because the deviant cannot overcome the proper. Devils and spirits cannot disturb me.

I have faith that the Buddhas and Bodhisattvas protect my Dharma at all times. Wherever I go, although I encounter tremendous obstacles, they have no effect. Accidents do not occur. Everywhere, the inauspicious becomes auspicious. Due to the aid of Buddhas and Bodhisattvas, everything is calm and peaceful.

Wherever I went on this trip to Asia, I met people every day who sought cures for their illnesses. The causes of their illnesses were always serious karmic obstructions. If they'd had no such obstructions, they would never have caught their strange diseases.

195

怪的病，中西醫皆束手無策，無法醫治的絕症。
生怪病的人，在過去生中，多數貪便宜，不肯吃
虧；或者吝嗇成性，一毛不拔，不肯布施救濟窮
人，處處為自己著想，不為大家著想，時時自私
自利，見利忘義，所以搞得業障一天比一天重，
終於生了怪病。

還有，患怪病的人，在往昔曾毀謗三寶，甚至謗
大乘經，所以墮落在地獄受苦。從地獄出來，再
轉為畜生，或為飛禽、或為走獸。做完畜生，再
轉做人，可是做人時，多數六根不全，有種種的
缺陷，或是瞎子、或是聾子、或是啞吧、或是瘸
子，總而言之，生理不健全。這類的人，在往昔
造了惡業，所以今生受這種果報。

受這種果報的人，本應該生大懺悔心，多做功德
事，才是對的。可惜他們不但不覺悟，而且愛財
如命，想在出家人身上找便宜。求我治病，還想
貪便宜，希望不要花錢，就能治好病。病好之後
，很慷慨地封一個紅包，做為供養。可是紅包內
只有一塊錢（新加坡或馬來西亞錢），或者兩塊

All the people who came to see me did so because of unusual diseases, problems that neither Asian nor Western medicine could cure, such as cancers that would not respond to treatment. For the most part, these people with strange illnesses had sought "bargains" in their past lives, and had been unwilling to take a loss. Perhaps they had been stingy penny-pinchers by nature, tightwads who wouldn't give a cent to help poor people, who thought exclusively of their own advantages. Such people never considered the welfare of others as important, but instead were constantly selfish out of personal indulgence. Hunger for profits obscured their good conscience; thus, their karmic obstacles increased daily, and eventually emerged in the form of an unusual illness.

People who contract curious diseases are invariably people who have slandered the Triple Jewel in past lives. They may even have slighted the Great Vehicle Sutras, an offense that can send people to the hells. Once they left the hells, they ascended to the realm of animals, where they may have been reborn as birds or beasts. Once their debts in the animal realm were repaid, they could be reborn as human beings. Reborn as a person, nonetheless, they invariably suffered birth defects—were paraplegic or otherwise disabled, blind or deaf, mute or lame—in general, they lacked a complete share of humanity. People such as these created evil karma in the past, and so in this life they are undergoing these kinds of retribution.

People who receive these kinds of retributions ought to be deeply ashamed and remorseful. They should busily earn more merit and virtue. That would be the right thing to do. Unfortunately, they fail to realize this and love money more than their own lives. They expect to get a quick bargain from this left-home person. They come demanding that I heal them, yet still seek a bargain, hoping to

錢，至多五塊錢。他們業障這樣重，還想貪便宜，這是多麼地可憐！

我為什麼對各位說這件事呢？因為要令各位提高警覺，謹慎小心，不可造惡業。在佛教裏不可誹謗三寶，不可謗大乘經，不可狐疑不修行，不可妄語欺騙人。如果造這種種的惡業，將來一定會墮落地獄。到時候，做師父的也是愛莫能助，無法援救。我事先聲明了，免得屆時埋怨師父不救你出地獄。

be completely cured without spending a penny. When their illness is better, they "generously" donate a red envelope as an offering. The envelope will most often contain one dollar (Singapore or Malaysian currency), or perhaps two dollars, but never more than five dollars. Even with karmic burdens as heavy as theirs, they are still greedy for petty profits. How pitiful!

Why have I related this to all of you? In order to alert you to the need for caution. You must not create bad karma, nor can you slander the Triple Jewel of Buddhism. You must not slander Great Vehicle Sutras. Do not hang on to doubts that keep you from cultivating; do not tell lies and cheat people. Evil karma such as this will certainly send you to the hells. Then in the future, even if your teacher wants to help you, he can't, because you'll be beyond salvation. I'm telling you in advance, so that when the time comes, you won't complain that your teacher didn't come and rescue you from the hells.

圖：江逸子居士提供　Picture provided by:Upasaka Jiang Yizi

貪著境界會招魔

參禪的人，應該要無著無貪。

「參禪」這一法，要腳踏實地參，埋頭苦幹地修
，勇猛向前進，絕不向後退。有這種的恆心，才
是真正的參禪人。

在參禪時，要用忍耐心來克服一切疼，腿痛不管
它，腰痠不理它。要想開悟，就得忍耐：不能忍
耐，就不能開悟。這個忍，包括忍飢、忍渴、忍
寒、忍痛，一切都要忍耐。若是能忍，就破除我
執。若沒有一個我的執著，向內觀心，心也沒有
了；向外觀形，形也沒有了；向遠觀一切物，物
也沒有了。這時，內無身心，外無世界，這就是
一個空。

這個空，還不能執著它，如有一個空的存在，那
還是一種執著。要把空也沒有了，才能與法界合

200

Attachment to States Leads to Demonic Possession

Cultivators of Chan should be free of greed and attachment.

This method of Chan meditation requires that as we meditate, we adopt a down-to-earth attitude. We have to cultivate with our "nose to the grindstone," so to speak. We have to be courageous as we advance. We absolutely may not retreat. With this persevering attitude, we are qualified to be called true Chan meditators.

As we meditate Chan-style, we use patience to overcome all pain. If our legs hurt, we pay no attention. If our back aches, we pay it no mind. If you really want to get enlightened, you have to be patient. If you can't be patient, then you can't get enlightened. The patience that I am talking about includes patience with hunger, patience with thirst, cold, and pain. You have to endure all these different trials. If you can endure them, then you can break through attachment to a self. If you have no attachment to a self, then when you look inside to contemplate your mind, you won't find it. When you look outside to contemplate your body, your body is also gone. When you look afar at all the different things in the universe, none of those things exist either. That's the time when "inside you find no body and mind, and outside you find no world." This is a state of emptiness.

This emptiness, however, is not something to become attached to. If you still hang on to an emptiness, then you are still clinging. Only

而爲一，與虛空沒有什麼分別。這種境界到了極點，就是一個定。在定中，不是糊糊塗塗的，而是明明白白的，所謂「如如不動，了了常明。」不是說，我坐禪有所企圖，貪著有個什麼境界現前。如果有這種妄想，便會招魔來擾亂。

在《金剛經》上說：

> 凡所有相。皆是虛妄。
> 若見諸相非相。即見如來。

所以參禪的人，不能執著境界的存在，更不要貪著神通；若有貪著，便會走火入魔。也不要貪著虛妄的名利，否則會走入旁門左道，成爲魔王的眷屬。這實在是可怕之至！我們參禪的人，應該要無著無貪，所以才說：

> 佛來佛斬，魔來魔斬。

用金剛王寶劍（智慧）斬斷一切，好的境界不貪，壞的境界更不貪。千萬不要貪小小的境界，認爲這是功夫，那會誤入歧途，不可不愼！

if you can get rid of emptiness as well, can you become one with, and the same as, the Dharma Realm. You will not be different in any way from empty space. When this state reaches an ultimate point, you'll attain samadhi. Within samadhi, you are not confused and muddled; you are extremely clear and sharp. We call it a state of being "Thus, thus unmoving; understanding, and constantly aware." It's not that when I sit in meditation, I chart out a plan, I have a motive, and I'm greedy for a state to occur. If you have these vain thoughts, you'll be disturbed by demons.

In the *Vajra Sutra* it says,

> *All appearances are false.*
> *If you can see all appearances as false,*
> *Then you'll see the Tathagata.*

Therefore, people who meditate cannot attach to states, nor do they want to get greedily attached to spiritual powers. As soon as you have an attachment, you can be possessed by a demon. Nor do you want to be greedy for and attach to phony fame and profit. Otherwise, you can easily run afoul of cults, or join the followers of demons, and that's something you should fear to the extreme. Cultivators of Chan should be unattached and free of greed. That's why we say,

> *When the Buddha comes, slay the Buddha;*
> *When the demons come, slay the demons.*

Use your royal Vajra-jeweled sword (wisdom) to slice through everything. Don't crave good states, and even less should you crave bad states. By no means should you crave tiny states and assume that they are signs of spiritual skill. If you do, you will surely go down the wrong road. You must not be careless at all.

203

打禪七時，把我忘了，把人忘了，把時間忘了，把空間也忘了。所謂「掃一切法，離一切相」，什麼也不執著，一切放下，這時候，便能進入四禪天的境界。

During the period of our meditation retreat, you must forget yourself, forget other people, forget about time and space. That is to say, "Sweep out all dharmas. Leave all marks and attachments behind." Don't attach yourself to anything; put everything down. At that time you will be able to enter into states of the Four Dhyana Heavens.

四禪天的境界

一念不生全體現，六根忽動被雲遮。

參禪參到忘人無我的境界，便到初禪「離生喜樂地」。在這個階段，破了眾生的執著，而得到禪悅為食，法喜充滿的受用。在此定的境界上，呼吸停止，無呼無吸，不出不入，有一種特別的快樂。這種快樂，是妙不可言的，總之，這是一般人得不到的快樂。

二禪是「定生喜樂地」，在定中得到最大的歡喜。坐在那裏，不飲不食。脈搏也停止，等於死人一樣，可是還有意念，知道自己在靜坐。

三禪是「離喜妙樂地」，在定中離開禪悅為食、法喜充滿這種的歡喜，而得到一種妙樂。這種妙樂，沒有法子可以形容，是微妙不可思議的。在

206

The States of the Four Dhyana Heavens

When not even one thought arises, the entire substance appears. But when the six sense organs suddenly move, you're covered by clouds.

When you as a Chan cultivator enter into a state where you forget yourself and forget others, you have reached the stage of the First Dhyana, which is called the Stage of the Happiness of Leaving Birth. At this stage, you have broken away from the attachments of living beings and experience the feeling of "taking Dhyana bliss as food and being filled with the joy of Dharma." In this samadhi, your breath will have stopped; you will no longer inhale or exhale. There is a unique happiness that is wonderful and inexpressible. This happiness is one that most people never experience.

The Second Dhyana is called the Stage of the Happiness of Producing Samadhi. In this samadhi, you experience the greatest joy. When you're sitting, you don't want to eat or drink. Your pulse has stopped. You're just like a dead person, but you still have thoughts and you are aware that you are sitting in meditation.

The Third Dhyana is the Stage of the Wonderful Bliss of Leaving Happiness. In this stage of samadhi, you leave the happiness of "taking Dhyana bliss as food and being filled with the joy of Dharma" and attain a kind of wonderful bliss that is impossible to describe. It's subtle and inconceivable. In this particular state, your thoughts have stopped. You have no thoughts. It's been described

此境界，把念頭也止住了，沒有意念，所謂「一念不生全體現，六根忽動被雲遮。」

四禪是「捨念清淨地」，到了這個境界，意念不但止住，而且也捨了。這時候，得到非常清淨、非常微妙的快樂。四禪的境界，還是凡夫的地位，尚未證果，不要以爲了不起。此境界離證果尚有一段距離，應該努力去參，再接再厲去參，進一步才到「五不還天」的境界，那才是入聖人法性流。

有個無聞比丘，他參到四禪的境界，誤認爲證了果位，所以到處宣傳，自己證了果。因爲他對佛法不徹底了解的緣故，所以打妄語，最後墮於無間地獄。

as: "When not even one thought arises, the entire substance appears. But when the six sense organs suddenly move, you're covered by clouds."

The Fourth Dhyana is the Stage of the Purity of Renouncing Thought. When you reach this state, not only are your thoughts stopped, they are eliminated entirely. At this time, you attain an extremely pure and wonderfully subtle joy. However, the state of the Fourth Dhyana is still at the stage of a common mortal. You have not yet realized fruition of your cultivation. Do not assume you are a special person, because you're still far from realizing the fruition. You should still work hard at your cultivation and meditate diligently, because if you can advance, you'll reach the state of the Five Heavens of No Return. That's when you enter the Dharma-nature stream of sages.

There was a person known as the Unlearned Bhikshu, who had cultivated to the stage of the Fourth Dhyana, but mistakenly assumed that he had realized the fruition of Arhatship. He went about announcing that he had realized the fruition. Because he did not have a thorough understanding of the Buddhadharma, he uttered a major lie and later fell into the uninterrupted hells.

參禪的祕訣

在自己的自性上用功夫，
不是向外馳求。

禪譯為「靜慮」，又為「思惟修」。思惟就是參；靜慮就是「時時勤拂拭，勿使惹塵埃」。思惟修就是教你提起話頭，念茲在茲，時刻不忘的意思。所謂「朝於斯，夕於斯」，在自己的自性上用功夫，不是向外馳求。凡是外來的境界，若是跟著它跑，便很容易走錯路。從自性生出的境界，才是真境界。這一點，希望各位要弄清楚，否則便上魔王的當，結果成了他的眷屬。

靜慮這個法門，要綿綿密密地用功，不要間斷。在用功的時候，要好像母雞在孵蛋那樣地專心，又好像龍在養珠那樣地謹慎，又好像貓在捕鼠那樣地忍耐。參禪要有堅、誠、恆的心，不可有驕傲的心。不要以為我比誰都高，比誰都強。如果有這種思想，那就是狂魔入體，功夫不會進步。

The Secret to Success in Chan Meditation

You should apply effort within your own nature and not seek outside.

Chan translates as "stilling the thought." It also means "thought cultivation." "Thought" refers to investigating the meditation topic. "Stilling the thought" means, "At all times, wipe it clean, and let no dust alight." "Thought cultivation" is done by means of raising the meditation topic in thought after thought and never forgetting it. As it is said, "We do it in the morning, and we also do it in the evening." You should apply effort within your own nature and not seek outside. If you follow after any external state, it is easy to go astray. Only states that arise from your own nature are true states. I hope all of you will note this point clearly. Otherwise, you will be tricked by the demon king and end up as one of his followers.

This Dharma-door of "stilling the thought" requires that you apply continuous, unrelenting effort, without any interruption. In your meditation, you should as concentrated as a mother hen sitting on her eggs. You should also be as careful as a dragon guarding its pearl. Furthermore, you must be as patient as a cat waiting outside a mousehole. Chan meditation requires determination, sincerity, and perseverance. You cannot be arrogant and assume that you're higher and better than everyone else. If you have thoughts like these, that means a demon of insanity has possessed you, and your skill will never advance.

參禪的時候，不可打妄想。打妄想就沒有真實的受用，浪費大好的時光。參禪要有忍耐心、長遠心。參禪的祕訣，就是忍，忍不住也要忍；忍到極點，就豁然貫通，明朗開悟。若沒有忍耐心，不能吃得苦，不能耐得勞，遇到境界，便投降了，這種行為最要不得，是參禪的大忌。

When you cultivate Chan, you should not indulge in idle thoughts. When you have idle thoughts, you don't gain any benefit, and you waste a tremendous amount of time. Sitting in Chan requires patience and perseverance. The secret of success in Chan meditation is patience; whatever you cannot endure, you must still endure. If you can endure to the ultimate point, then suddenly you can penetrate through and experience the clarity of enlightenment. If you lack patience and cannot endure bitterness and fatigue, then you will surrender to the states that you encounter. To give in like that is a great mistake; it is the great taboo in Chan meditation!

金剛王寶劍斬妄想

為什麼不能成佛？就因為妄想執著。

妄想是開悟的絆腳石，參「念佛是誰？」就是一把金剛王寶劍，能斬斷一切的妄想。釋迦牟尼佛在菩提樹下，初成正覺時，便說：「奇哉！奇哉！大地眾生，無不具有如來智慧德相，但因妄想執著，不能證得。」佛明明白白地告訴我們，為什麼不能成佛？就因為妄想執著，所以要破妄想執著。如何破法呢？就用「誰」字，向下鑿，鑿到水落石出，便是成功時。

參禪，就是參這個「念佛是誰？」時時刻刻在腦海中研究這個問題，不間斷地研究。時間一長，自然有消息。所謂：

久坐有禪，久住有緣。

坐的時間久了，自然有禪。居住的時間久了，東

The Vajra-King Jeweled Sword Cuts Through Idle Thoughts

Why can't we become Buddhas? It's simply because of our idle thoughts and attachments.

Idle thoughts are a stumbling block to getting enlightened. Investigating "Who is reciting the Buddha's name?" is a Vajra-king jeweled sword which can cut through all idle thoughts. When Shakyamuni Buddha first accomplished Right Enlightenment beneath the Bodhi Tree, he said, "How strange, how strange! All living beings, without exception, possess the wisdom and virtuous characteristics of the Tathagata (the Buddha). It is because of their idle thoughts and attachments that they cannot certify to them." The Buddha clearly told us why we can't become Buddhas. It's simply because of our idle thoughts and attachments. So we must break through these idle thoughts and attachments. How do we break through them? We use the word "Who?" We drill down into it, drilling until the truth is brought to light. That's when we succeed.

When we meditate, we are investigating the question, "Who is reciting the Buddha's name?" At all times, in the ocean of our consciousness, we look into this question without cease. After doing this for a long time, there will naturally be good news. It's said,

After we sit for a long time, Chan will appear.
After dwelling somewhere for a long time,
  we will have affinities.

215

鄰西舍自然有緣份，情感融洽，和平相處。參禪
參到火候時，不但沒有妄想，而且脾氣小了，煩
惱少了，人品高了，氣度也大了。這時候，智慧
現前，明白是非，辨別善惡，把貪瞋癡清理得乾
乾淨淨，只有戒定慧大放光明，照見五蘊皆空。

After sitting for a long enough time, we will experience the states of Chan. And when we live somewhere long enough, we develop affinities with our neighbors. We will share a harmonious relationship and live peacefully together.

When we have investigated Chan to the point that our skill is close to perfection, not only will we be free of idle thoughts, but our temper will also be smaller, our afflictions will be fewer, our personality will be noble, and our mind capacity will also be great. At that time, wisdom will come forth. We will understand how to tell right from wrong. We will be able to clearly discriminate between good and evil. We will have washed clean our greed, hatred, and stupidity, so that only the light of precepts, concentration, and wisdom remains, revealing that the Five Aggregates are all empty.

迴向偈

願以此功德　　莊嚴佛淨土
上報四重恩　　下濟三途苦
若有見聞者　　悉發菩提心
盡此一報身　　同生極樂國

Verse of Transference

May the merit and virtue accrued from this work
Adorn the Buddhas' Pure Lands,
Repaying four kinds of kindness above
And aiding those suffering in the paths below.
May those who see and hear of this
All bring forth the resolve for Bodhi
And, when this retribution body is over,
Be born together in the Land of Ultimate Bliss.

附錄
Appendix

辭彙解釋 ❏
Glossary

宣化上人簡傳 ❏
Biographical Sketch of the
Venerable Master Hsuan Hua

宣化上人十八大願 ❏
The Eighteen Great Vows of
the Venerable Master Hua

Glossary

This glossary is an aid for readers unfamiliar with the Buddhist vocabulary. Definitions have been kept simple, and are not necessarily complete.

Amitabha Buddha 阿彌陀佛 The Buddha of the Land of Ultimate Bliss.

Arhat 阿羅漢 One of the fruitions of the path of cultivation. Arhats have ended the birth and death of the body.

Asura 阿修羅 Asuras are beings who like to fight. They may live in the heavens, among people, in the animal realm, or as ghosts.

Bhikshu 比丘 A fully ordained Buddhist monk, one who leads a pure and celibate life and upholds 250 precepts.

Bodhi 菩提 Enlightenment.

Bodhisattva 菩薩 An enlightened being who does not enter Nirvana but chooses instead to remain in the world and save living beings.

Buddha 佛 The Enlightened One; one who has reached the Utmost, Right, and Equal Enlightenment.

Buddhadharma 佛法 Methods of cultivation taught by the Buddha leading beings to enlightenment.

Buddha-nature 佛性 The potential for Buddhahood inherent in all beings.

Chan 禪 One of the five major schools of Buddhism. The teaching of meditation. Also, the Chinese transliteration of Dhyana.

Chan session 禪七 A retreat, usually lasting a multiple of seven days, during which participants practice sitting and walking meditation all day long.

cultivation 修行 The practical application of the methods taught by the Buddha that lead to enlightenment.

Dharma 法 The teachings of the Buddha. After the Buddha's Nirvana, the Dharma passes through the following historical periods:

1. The first 1000 years is the Proper Dharma Age
2. The following 1,000 years is the Dharma Image Age
3. The following 10,000 years is the Dharma-ending Age

dharma 法 An element of psycho-physical existence; a method of cultivation.

Dharma-door 法門 An entrance to the Dharma, a method of practice leading to enlightenment.

Dharma-ending Age 末法時代 See Dharma.

Dharma Master 法師 A teacher of Dharma. A respectful term of address for members of the Sangha.

Dharma-protector 護法 Lay supporters of the Buddhist monastic establishment; also the gods, spirits, and ghosts who protect the Dharma and those who cultivate it.

Dharma Realm 法界 The enlightened world, that is, the totality or infinity of the realm of the Buddhas; a particular plane of existence, as in the Ten Dharma Realms.

Dhyana 禪 A practice of thought cultivation and insight which leads to the development of higher mental states.

externalist way 外道 Heterodox sect.

Five Spiritual Eyes 五戒 The five are the Flesh Eye, the Heavenly Eye, the Dharma Eye, the Wisdom Eye, and the Buddha Eye. These non-corporeal 'eyes' are possessed by the Buddhas and other enlightened beings. They can also begin to function in people who are not enlightened, but who are cultivating or who have cultivated in past lives.

five precepts 五戒 The five lay precepts are: no killing, no stealing, no sexual misconduct, no false speech, and no intoxicants.

Guanshiyin/Guanyin Bodhisattva 觀世音菩薩 The Bodhisattva of Great Compassion Who Regards the Sounds of the World. "Guanshiyin" is a Chinese transliteration of the Bodhisattva's Sanskrit name, Avalokiteshvara.

Hearers 聲聞 The Buddha's disciples who hear the sound of the Buddha's voice and awaken to the Way (Sanskrit: Shravaka).

karma 業 Deeds, activity. Karma does not mean fate. It means the deeds which we create ourselves and the retributions which those deeds bring upon us.

Land of Ultimate Bliss 極樂世界 The Buddhaland of Amitabha Buddha in the West created through the power of his vows which enable living beings to be reborn simply by constant mindfulness and recitation of his name. Also known as the Western Pure Land.

leave home 出家 To renounce the householder's life and become a monk or nun in order to devote oneself completely to the practice of the Buddhadharma.

Manjushri Bodhisattva 文殊師利菩薩 Manjushri is a Sanskrit word meaning "Wonderful Virtue" or "Wonderfully Auspicious." He is the eldest of the great Bodhisattvas and has the greatest wisdom.

Nirvana 涅槃 Perfect quiescence realized by enlightened sages.

outflows 漏 All bad habits and faults are outflows. Outflows are the root of birth and death; they let our vital energy leak away.

Prajna 般若 Transcendental wisdom. Prajna Paramita means "the perfection of wisdom."

Saha World 娑婆世界 The name of the world we live in. "Saha" means "able to endure"; beings of this world are capable of bearing much suffering.

samadhi 三昧 A wholesome state of concentration gained through meditation and other practices; there are various kinds of samadhi.

Samantabhadra (Universal Worthy) Bodhisattva 普賢菩薩 One of the greatest of the Bodhisattvas. He is renowned as foremost in conduct.

Sangha 僧伽 The community of Buddhist monks and nuns.

six paths of rebirth 六道 See Ten Dharma Realms.

six spiritual powers 六種神通 The heavenly eye, heavenly ear, knowledge of previous lives, knowledge of the minds of others, complete spirit, and elimination of outflows.

Skandhas 陰 Constituents of the entire psycho-physical unit which we mistake for a personality. The Five Skandhas are form, feelings, thoughts, activities, and consciousness.

Sutra 經 Discourses by the Buddha or by various members of the assembly with the authority of the Buddha.

Tathagata 如來 A title of the Buddha meaning "Thus Come One."

Ten Dharma Realms 十法界 The four realms of the sages (Buddhas, Bodhisattvas, Those Enlightened to Conditions, and Hearers) and the six paths of rebirth (gods, humans, asuras, animals, hungry ghosts, and hell-beings).

ten good deeds 十善 Abstention from: killing, stealing, sexual misconduct, duplicity, harsh speech, lying, irrresponsible speech, greed, anger, and stupidity.

Those Enlightened to Conditions 緣覺 Those who attain enlightenment through contemplating the links of conditioned co-production (Sanskrit: Pratyekabuddha).

three evil paths 三惡道 The realms of animals, hungry ghosts, and hell-beings.

three poisons 三毒 Greed, hatred, and stupidity.

Three Treasuries 三藏 The Sutras, the Vinaya (precepts and rules), and the Shastras (treatises).

Triple Jewel 三寶 The Buddha, the Dharma, and the Sangha.

Triple Realm 三界 The Realm of Desire, the Realm of Form, and the Formless Realm.

Vajra 金剛 A Sanskrit word which means "durable," "luminous," and "able to cut." It is indestructible and is usually represented by diamond.

The Way 道 The spiritual path of cultivation; the ultimate truth, which is realized through following that path.

Way-place 道場 A monastery; a place where enlightenment is sought and attained.

宣化上人簡傳

上人，法名安慈，字度輪，接雲公法，爲禪宗潙仰派第九代傳人，法號宣化，又號「墓中僧」。吉林省雙城縣人，清末戊午年三月十六日生。俗姓白，父富海，母胡氏。上人的母親一生茹素念佛，懷上人時曾向佛菩薩祈願，生上人前夕，夢見阿彌陀佛大放光明，遂生上人。

幼年時代，上人隨母親茹素念佛，年十一，見生死事大，無常迅速，毅然有出家之志，十五歲皈依上常下智老和尚爲師。十九歲母親逝世，禮請三緣寺上常下智老和尚爲剃度，披緇結廬於母墓旁，守孝期間，拜華嚴、禮淨懺、修禪定、習教觀，嚴守日中一食，功夫日純，得到鄉里人民的愛戴禮敬，其洗鍊精虔，感動諸佛菩薩、護法龍天，故靈異之事多不勝數，神異事蹟廣傳，被稱爲奇僧。

一九四六年，因慕虛雲老和尚爲宗門泰斗，乃前

224

Biographical Sketch of the Venerable Master Hsuan Hua

The Venerable Master, whose Dharma name is An Tse and style name is Du Lun, received the Dharma from the Venerable Master Hsu Yun and became the Ninth Patriarch of the Wei Yang Lineage. His name is Hsuan Hua, and he is also called The Monk in the Grave. A native of Shuangcheng County of Jilin Province, he was born on the sixteenth day of the third lunar month in the year of Wu Wu at the end of the Qing Dynasty. His father's name was Bai Fuhai. His mother, whose maiden name was Hu, ate only vegetarian food and recited the Buddha's name throughout her life. When she was pregnant with the Master, she prayed to the Buddhas and Bodhisattvas. The night before his birth, in a dream, she saw Amitabha Buddha emitting brilliant light. Following that the Master was born.

As a child, the Master followed his mother's example by eating only vegetarian food and reciting the Buddha's name. At the age of eleven, he became aware of the great matter of birth and death and the brevity of life, and he resolved to leave the home-life. At fifteen, he took refuge under the Venerable Master Chang Zhi. When he was nineteen, his mother passed away, and he requested Venerable Master Chang Zhi of Sanyuan Temple to shave his head. Dressed in the left-home robes, he built a simple hut by his mother's grave and observed the practice of filial piety. During that period, he bowed to the *Avatamsaka Sutra,* performed worship and pure repentance, practiced Chan meditation, studied the teachings and contemplations, and strictly kept the rule of eating only one meal at midday. As his skill grew ever more pure, he won the admiration and respect of the villagers. His intensely sincere efforts to purify and cultivate himself moved the Buddhas and Bodhisattvas as well

往參禮。虛雲老和尚觀其為法門龍象,乃傳授其法脈,為溈仰宗第九代接法人,為摩訶迦葉初祖傳承的四十六代。

一九四八年,叩別虛雲老和尚,赴香港弘法,闡揚禪、教、律、密、淨五宗並重,打破門戶之見。並重建古剎、印經造像,分別成立西樂園寺、佛教講堂、慈興寺,開演經典多部,使佛法大興於香江。

一九五九年,師觀察西方機緣成熟,為將佛教的真實義理傳到世界各地,遂令弟子在美成立中美佛教總會〔後改為法界佛教總會〕。一九六二年,應美國佛教人士邀請,隻身赴美,樹正法幢於三藩市佛教講堂。

一九六八年,成立暑假楞嚴講修班,數十名華盛頓州立大學學生,遠來學習佛法。結業後,美籍青年五人,懇求剃度出家,創下美國佛教史始有僧相的記錄。此後,在上人座下披剃的美國弟子

as the Dharma-protecting gods and dragons. The miraculous responses were too many to be counted. As news of these supernatural events spread far and wide, the Master came to be regarded as a remarkable monk.

Esteeming the Venerable Master Hsu Yun as a great hero of Buddhism, the Master went to pay homage to him in 1946. The Venerable Master Hsu Yun saw that the Master would become an outstanding figure in the Dharma, and transmitted the Dharma-pulse to him, making him the Ninth Patriarch of the Wei Yang Lineage, the forty-sixth generation since the Patriarch Mahakashyapa.

In 1948, the Master bid farewell to the Venerable Master Hsu Yun and went to Hong Kong to propagate the Dharma. He gave equal importance to the five schools—Chan, Doctrine, Vinaya, Esoteric, and Pure Land—thus putting an end to prejudice towards any particular sect. The Master also renovated old temples, printed Sutras and constructed images. He established Western Bliss Garden Monastery, the Buddhist Lecture Hall, and Cixing Monastery. Delivering lectures on numerous Sutras, the Master caused Buddhism to flourish in Hong Kong.

In 1959, the Master saw that conditions were ripe in the West, and he instructed his disciples to establish the Sino-American Buddhist Association (later renamed the Dharma Realm Buddhist Association) in the United States. In 1962, at the invitation of American Buddhists, the Master traveled alone to the United States, where he raised the banner of proper Dharma at the Buddhist Lecture Hall in San Francisco.

In 1968, the Shurangama Study and Practice Summer Session was held, and several dozen students from the University of Washington in Seattle came to study the Buddhadharma. After the session was concluded, five young Americans requested permission to shave

日多，對佛法弘揚於西方及翻譯經典，都帶來深遠的影響。

上人講經說法，深入淺出，數十年如一日，升座說法萬餘次，現已有百餘種譯爲英文，爲佛經譯爲英文最多者。一九七三年成立國際譯經學院，預計將《大藏經》譯成各國文字，使佛法傳遍寰宇。

一九七四年，購置萬佛聖城，成立法界佛教大學、僧伽居士訓練班，培育國際性佛學專才。又創辦育良小學、培德中學，以教育來挽救人心。數年來相繼成立金山聖寺、金輪聖寺、金峰聖寺、金佛聖寺、華嚴聖寺、法界聖寺、彌陀聖寺、法界聖城等正法道場多處。上人本著捨己爲人之精神，不辭勞苦，以身作則，辦校演教，提拔後秀，獻出萬佛聖城爲「全世界佛教徒皈依處」。萬佛聖城家風嚴峻，堅守上人自出家以來的六大宗旨：不爭、不貪、不求、不自私、不自利、不打妄語的原則。由於上人人格與修行的感召，萬佛聖城已成爲美國佛教重要的道場。

their heads and leave the home-life, marking the beginning of the Sangha in the history of American Buddhism. Since then, the number of American disciples who have left the home-life under the Venerable Master has continued to grow, creating a profound and far-reaching impact on the propagation of the Buddhadharma and the translation of Sutras in the West.

The Master's explanations of Sutras and lectures on Dharma are profound and yet easy to understand. Several decades have passed in a flash, and the Master has ascended the Dharma seat and delivered well over ten thousand Dharma lectures. Over a hundred of his explanations have been translated into English. No one else has overseen the translation of so many Sutras into English. In 1973 the Master established the International Translation Institute, which plans to translate the entire Buddhist Canon into the languages of every country, so that the Buddhadharma will spread throughout the world.

In 1974, the Master purchased the City of Ten Thousand Buddhas and established the Dharma Realm Buddhist University and the Sangha and Laity Training Programs in order to train Buddhist professionals on an international scale. Furthermore, he founded Instilling Goodness Elementary School and Developing Virtue Secondary School in order to save children's minds from corruption. Over subsequent years, the Master has successively established Gold Mountain Monastery, Gold Wheel Monastery, Gold Summit Monastery, Gold Buddha Monastery, Avatamsaka Monastery, Dharma Realm Monastery, Amitabha Monastery, the City of the Dharma Realm, and other Way-places of the proper Dharma. Dedicating himself to serving others, the Master doesn't mind the toil and suffering. Acting as a model for others in founding schools and expounding the teachings, and in order to promote the talent of future generations, the Master has offered the City of Ten Thousand Buddhas as the "Refuge for the Buddhists of the World." The traditions at the City of Ten Thousand Buddhas

上人曾撰一聯以明其志：

　　　凍死不攀緣，
　　　餓死不化緣，
　　　窮死不求緣。
　　　隨緣不變，不變隨緣，
　　　抱定我們三大宗旨。

　　　捨命爲佛事，
　　　造命爲本事，
　　　正命爲僧事。
　　　即事明理，明理即事，
　　　推行祖師一脈心傳。

上人甚深的禪定與智慧，實爲末法眾生開出菩提
大道，猶如在黑夜中見般若之燈，在黑暗裏聞法
嗣之香，在污泥穢地間開起清淨之蓮，令人動容
讚歎，知道偉大的修行人不可思議。

are strict, and residents vigorously strive to practice the Six Great Principles established by the Master after he left the home-life: do not contend, do not be greedy, do not seek, do not be selfish, do not pursue personal gain, and do not tell lies. Due to the influence of the Venerable Master's integrity and cultivation, the City of Ten Thousand Buddhas has become an important Buddhist Way-place in the United States. The Master has composed a verse expressing his principles:

Freezing to death, we do not scheme.
Starving to death, we do not beg.
Dying of poverty, we ask for nothing.
According with conditions, we do not change.
Not changing, we accord with conditions.
We adhere firmly to our three great principles.

We renounce our lives to do the Buddha's work.
We take the responsibility to mold our own destinies.
We rectify our lives as the Sangha's work.
Encountering specific matters,
  we understand the principles.
Understanding the principles,
  we apply them in specific matters.
We carry on the single pulse of the patriarchs'
  mind-transmission.

The Venerable Master's profound samadhi and wisdom have truly opened up the great way of Bodhi for living beings in the age of the Dharma's decline. It is as if in the dark night, we suddenly see the lamp of Prajna wisdom; and in the obscurity, we smell the fragrance of the Dharma lineage. It is like a pure lotus which grows out of the mud and blooms. Upon realizing the inconceivable state of a great cultivator, we are moved to express our praise and exaltation.

231

宣化上人十八大願

一、願盡虛空、遍法界、十方三世一切菩薩等，
　　若有一未成佛時，我誓不取正覺。

二、願盡虛空、遍法界、十方三世一切緣覺等，
　　若有一未成佛時，我誓不取正覺。

三、願盡虛空、遍法界、十方三世一切聲聞等，
　　若有一未成佛時，我誓不取正覺。

四、願三界諸天人等，若有一未成佛時，我誓不
　　取正覺。

五、願十方世界一切人等，若有一未成佛時，我
　　誓不取正覺。

六、願天、人、一切阿修羅等，若有一未成佛時
　　，我誓不取正覺。

七、願一切畜生界等，若有一未成佛時，我誓不
　　取正覺。

八、願一切餓鬼界等，若有一未成佛時，我誓不
　　取正覺。

The Eighteen Great Vows of the Venerable Master Hua

1. I vow that as long as there is a single Bodhisattva in the three periods of time throughout the ten directions of the Dharma Realm, to the very end of empty space, who has not accomplished Buddhahood, I too will not attain the right enlightenment.

2. I vow that as long as there is a single Pratyekabuddha in the three periods of time throughout the ten directions of the Dharma Realm, to the very end of empty space, who has not accomplished Buddhahood, I too will not attain the right enlightenment.

3. I vow that as long as there is a single Shravaka in the three periods of time throughout the ten directions of the Dharma Realm, to the very end of empty space, who has not accomplished Buddhahood, I too will not attain the right enlightenment.

4. I vow that as long as there is a single god in the Triple Realm who has not accomplished Buddhahood, I too will not attain the right enlightenment.

5. I vow that as long as there is a single human being in the worlds of the ten directions who has not accomplished Buddhahood, I too will not attain the right enlightenment.

6. I vow that as long as there is a single asura who has not accomplished Buddhahood, I too will not attain the right enlightenment.

7. I vow that as long as there is a single animal who has not accomplished Buddhahood, I too will not attain the right enlightenment.

8. I vow that as long as there is a single hungry ghost who has not accomplished Buddhahood, I too will not attain the right enlightenment.

233

九、願一切地獄界等，若有一未成佛，或地獄不空時，我誓不取正覺。

十、願凡是三界諸天、仙、人、阿修羅，飛潛動植、靈界龍畜、鬼神等眾，曾經皈依我者，若有一未成佛時，我誓不取正覺。

十一、願將我所應享受一切福樂，悉皆迴向，普施法界眾生。

十二、願將法界眾生所有一切苦難，悉皆與我一人代受。

十三、願分靈無數，普入一切不信佛法眾生心，令其改惡向善，悔過自新，皈依三寶，究竟作佛。

十四、願一切眾生，見我面，乃至聞我名，悉發菩提心，速得成佛道。

十五、願恪遵佛制，實行日中一食。

十六、願覺諸有情，普攝群機。

十七、願此生即得五眼六通，飛行自在。

十八、願一切求願，必獲滿足。

結云：

> 眾生無邊誓願度，
> 煩惱無盡誓願斷，
> 法門無量誓願學，
> 佛道無上誓願成。

9. I vow that as long as there is a single hell-dweller who has not accomplished Buddhahood, I too will not attain the right enlightenment.

10. I vow that as long as there is a single god, immortal, human, asura, air-bound or water-bound creature, animate or inanimate object, or a single dragon, beast, ghost, or spirit, etc., of the spiritual realm that has taken refuge with me and has not accomplished Buddhahood, I too will not attain the right enlightenment.

11. I vow to fully dedicate all blessings and bliss which I ought myself receive and enjoy to all living beings of the Dharma Realm.

12. I vow to fully take upon myself all sufferings and hardships of all the living beings in the Dharma Realm.

13. I vow to manifest innumerable bodies as a means to gain access into the minds of living beings throughout the universe who do not believe in the Buddhadharma, causing them to correct their faults and tend toward wholesomeness, repent of their errors and start anew, take refuge in the Triple Jewel, and ultimately accomplish Buddhahood.

14. I vow that all living beings who see my face or even hear my name will fix their thoughts on Bodhi and quickly accomplish the Buddha Way.

15. I vow to respectfully observe the Buddha's instructions and cultivate the practice of eating only one meal per day.

16. I vow to enlighten all sentient beings, universally responding to the multitude of differing potentials.

17. I vow to obtain the five eyes, six spiritual powers, and the freedom of being able to fly in this very life.

18. I vow that all of my vows will certainly be fulfilled.

Conclusion:

I vow to save the innumerable living beings.
I vow to eradicate the inexhaustible afflictions.
I vow to study the illimitable Dharma-doors.
I vow to accomplish the unsurpassed Buddha Way.

南無護法韋陀菩薩
Namo Dharma Protector Wei Tuo Bodhisattva

法界佛教總會 · 萬佛聖城
Dharma Realm Buddhist Association
The City of Ten Thousand Buddhas
2001 Talmage Road, Talmage, CA 95481-0217 U.S.A.
Tel:(707)462-0939

法界聖城　The City of the Dharma Realm
1029 West Capitol Ave., West Sacramento, CA 95691 U.S.A.
Tel:(916)374-8268

國際譯經學院　The International Translation Institute
1777 Murchison Drive, Burlingame, CA 94010-4504 U.S.A.
Tel: (650)692-5912　Fax: (650)692-5056

法界宗教研究院（柏克萊寺）
Institute for World Religions (Berkeley Buddhist Monastery)
2304 McKinley Avenue, Berkeley, CA 94703 U.S.A.
Tel: (510)848-3440　Fax: (510)548-4551

金山聖寺　Gold Mountain Monastery
800 Sacramento Street, San Francisco, CA 94108 U.S.A.
Tel: (415)421-6117

金輪聖寺　Gold Wheel　Monastery
235 North Avenue 58, Los Angeles, CA 90042 U.S.A.
Tel: (213)258-6668

長堤聖寺　Long Beach Monastery
3361 East Ocean Boulevard, Long Beach, CA 90803 U.S.A.
Tel: (562)438-8902

金佛聖寺　Gold Buddha Monastery
301 East Hastings Street, Vancouver, BC V6A 1P3 CANADA
Tel: (604)684-3754

華嚴聖寺　Avatamsaka Monastery
1009-4th Avenue, S.W. Calgary, AB T2P 0K8 CANADA
Tel: (403)269-2960

法界佛教印經會
Dharma Realm Buddhist Books Distribution Society
臺灣省臺北市忠孝東路六段 85 號 11 樓
11th Floor, No.85, Sec. 6 Chung-Hsiao E. Road,
Taipei, Taiwan, R. O. C.
Tel: (02)2786-3022, 2786-2474　Fax: (02)2786-2674

紫雲洞觀音寺　Tze Yun Tung Temple
Batu 5 1/2, Jalan Sungai Besi, Salak Selatan,
57100 Kuala Lumpur, MALAYSIA.
Tel: (03)782-6560　Fax: (03)780-1272

宣化上人開示錄(四)

西曆二〇〇〇年三月廿四日 · 中英文版 · 平裝本
佛曆三〇二七年二月十九日 · 觀音菩薩聖誕

發 行 人　　法界佛教總會
出　　版　　法界佛教總會 · 佛經翻譯委員會 · 法界佛教大學
地　　址　　**Dharma Realm Buddhist Association &**
　　　　　　The City of Ten Thousand Buddhas
　　　　　　2001 Talmage Road, Talmage, CA 95481-0217　U.S.A.
　　　　　　電話：(707)462-0939　　傳眞：(707)462-0949

The International Translation Institute
1777 Murchison Drive Burlingame, CA 94010-4504 U.S.A.
電話：(650)692-5912　　傳眞：(650)692-5056

倡　　印　　萬佛聖城
　　　　　　The City of Ten Thousand Buddhas
　　　　　　2001 Talmage Road, Talmage, CA 95481-0217　U.S.A.
　　　　　　電話：(707)462-0939　　傳眞：(707)462-0949

ISBN-0-88139-028-3

●佛典所在，即佛所在，請恭敬尊重，廣爲流通。